100 Frequently Asked Questions about *Jesus Christ*

C. Austin Tucker

100 Frequently Asked Questions About Jesus Christ
by C. Austin Tucker
Copyright 2025. All rights reserved.

Except in the case of brief quotations embodied in critical articles and reviews, no portion of this book may be reproduced, stored in a retrieval system, or transmitted in any form or by any means—electronic, mechanical, photocopy, recording, scanning, or other—without prior written permission from the author.

For permission requests, write to the publisher at Publisher@Route66Ministries.com with "Attention: Permissions Coordinator" in the subject line.

Published by Route 66 Ministries.

TABLE OF CONTENTS

THE GOSPELS AND THEIR AUTHORSHIP 7

1. Can the Gospels be trusted? 7
2. Why do the Gospels tell different stories about Jesus? 9
3. Who wrote the four Gospels? 11
4. Who was the Gospel writer Matthew? 12
5. Who was the Gospel writer Mark? 12
6. Who was the Gospel writer Luke? 13
7. Who was the Gospel writer John? 14
8. Who is the "disciple Jesus loved" referred to in John's Gospel? 17
9. Why is John the only writer to record Lazarus' resurrection? 18

EARLY YEARS 21

10. When was Jesus born? 21
11. Why is Jesus' birth in Bethlehem significant? 22
12. Was Jesus really born in a manger/stable? 23
13. Why was there no room at the inn for Mary and Joseph? 23
14. Was Jesus circumcised? 24
15. Why wasn't Jesus called Immanuel in accordance with Isaiah 7:14 and Matthew 1:23? 24
16. Why are Matthew's and Luke's genealogies for Jesus so different? 25
17. Who was Herod? 27
18. Why did Herod the Great want Jesus killed as a baby? 30
19. Did Mary remain a virgin after giving birth to Jesus? 30
20. Is it important to believe that Jesus was born of a virgin? 31
21. Why is Jesus' childhood not recorded? 31
22. Did Jesus have siblings? 32

23. Who was John the Baptist? 33

DAILY LIFE 35
24. Why was Jesus baptized? 35
25. Did only one woman anoint Jesus' feet or was it two different women? 37
26. Why did Jesus write in the dirt when the adulterous woman was brought to him? 39
27. How long was Jesus' ministry on earth? 40
28. Why didn't Jesus stay on earth longer? 40
29. Did Jesus have a sense of humor? 41
30. Why is Jesus often referred to as Jesus of Nazareth? 42
31. What language did Jesus speak? 43
32. Was Jesus married? 43
33. Why was Jesus angry with the merchants in the temple? 44
34. How many times did Jesus cleanse the temple? 44
35. Where was Joseph during Jesus' ministry? 45
36. What did Jesus look like? 45
37. Who are all the Marys in the Gospels? 46
38. Why did Jesus curse the fig tree? 48
39. What was the transfiguration and why was it significant? 50

TEACHINGS AND DOCTRINE 51
40. Did Jesus teach that we shouldn't judge? 51
41. What is blasphemy against the Holy Spirit? 54
42. Aren't Christmas and Easter pagan holidays? 57
43. Why didn't Jesus discuss homosexuality? 66
44. What does it mean to be born again? 67
45. What did Jesus teach about divorce? 68
46. What did Jesus teach about paying taxes? 70
47. Why did the Pharisees hate Jesus? 71
48. Did Jesus teach against the Sabbath? 71
49. Did Jesus teach against the law? 75
50. What Old Testament prophecies about Christ were fulfilled? 78
51. Did Jesus ever sin? 86

52. Why did Jesus have to be tempted?........................ 87
53. Why did Jesus have to die? 87
54. Why is Jesus called the Son of David? 89
55. Why is Jesus called our High Priest? 90
56. Why did John call Jesus the Lamb of God? 91
57. Why are believers called Christians? 91
58. If Jesus was a Jew, why aren't Christians Jewish? .. 92

JESUS' DIVINITY 95

59. What does Philippians 2:5-11 mean when it states that Jesus emptied himself? 95
60. What is the relationship between Jesus and the archangel Michael? 96
61. If Jesus was born of a human, how did he escape humanity's sinful nature? 96
62. Did Jesus die for everyone? 97
63. What does it mean that Jesus was a little lower than the angels (Psalm 8:5; Hebrews 2:7)? 97
64. How can Jesus and the Bible both be the Word of God? 98
65. Why is Jesus' resurrection from the dead significant? 98
66. What is the significance of Jesus referring to himself as "I Am"? 99
67. What does it mean in John 3:16 that Jesus is God's only begotten son? 99
68. What are some other names and titles for Jesus Christ? 99
69. Why is Jesus called the second Adam? 100
70. What does Colossians 1:15-21 mean when it says that Jesus is the "firstborn" over creation? 101
71. Is the term "trinity" in the Bible? 101
72. What did Jesus mean when he identified himself as the resurrection and the life? 103
73. Is Jesus the only way to God? 103
74. Why is Jesus called Christ? 106
75. Why is Jesus called Lord? 107
76. Is Jesus God? 108
77. Why is Jesus called "the Word" in John 1:1? 114

- 78. IF JESUS IS GOD, WHY IS HE CALLED THE SON OF GOD?. 116
- 79. IF JESUS IS GOD, WHY IS HE CALLED THE SON OF MAN? 118
- 80. IF JESUS IS GOD, WHO DID HE PRAY TO? 119
- 81. IF JESUS IS GOD, WHY DIDN'T HE KNOW THE DATE OF HIS RETURN?.. 119
- 82. IF JESUS IS GOD, WHY DID HE SAY THE FATHER WAS GREATER THAN HE? 120
- 83. IF JESUS IS GOD, HOW COULD GOD FORSAKE HIM ON THE CROSS? 121
- 84. IF JESUS IS GOD, HOW COULD HE BE TEMPTED?........... 121
- 85. WHO RAISED JESUS FROM THE DEAD? 122

FINAL DAYS 125

- 86. WHAT WAS THE SEQUENCE OF EVENTS DURING THE LAST WEEK OF JESUS' DEATH? 125
- 87. WHY DID THE JEWISH LEADERS WANT TO KILL JESUS? ... 127
- 88. WHY DID THE JEWS GO TO PILATE INSTEAD OF KILLING JESUS THEMSELVES? 128
- 89. WHY DID JUDAS ISCARIOT BETRAY JESUS? 129
- 90. DID JUDAS GO TO HELL FOR BETRAYING JESUS? 130
- 91. WHO WAS RESPONSIBLE FOR JESUS' DEATH? 131
- 92. WAS THE LORD'S SUPPER A PASSOVER MEAL?............ 134
- 93. HOW LONG WAS JESUS ON THE CROSS? 136
- 94. DID JESUS GO TO HELL BETWEEN HIS DEATH AND RESURRECTION? 138
- 95. AT JESUS' DEATH, WHAT WAS THE SIGNIFICANCE OF THE VEIL OF THE TEMPLE BEING TORN IN HALF? 138
- 96. HOW LONG WAS JESUS IN THE TOMB? 139
- 97. WHO WERE THE WOMEN AT JESUS' CROSS/TOMB?...... 140
- 98. HOW MANY ANGELS WERE AT JESUS' TOMB?............. 141
- 99. IN WHAT ORDER DID JESUS APPEAR TO HIS FOLLOWERS AFTER HIS RESURRECTION?.. 142
- 100. WHY DIDN'T PEOPLE RECOGNIZE JESUS AFTER HE WAS RESURRECTED? 143

CONCLUSION 147

MORE BOOKS FROM C. AUSTIN TUCKER..................149

ABOUT C. AUSTIN TUCKER..153

CHAPTER ONE

THE GOSPELS AND THEIR AUTHORSHIP

1. CAN THE GOSPELS BE TRUSTED?

The four Gospels in the Bible are the first four books in the New Testament: **Matthew, Mark, Luke,** and **John.** And they tell four different, but complementary, versions of the life of Jesus Christ. Can they be trusted? Yes, absolutely.

Imagine the following scenario: You're famous and today you write a letter. Over the next 100 years, your letter is preserved in multiple ways: people photocopy it, copy it by hand, paraphrase it, and make notes on it. Within 200 years, your original copy is lost, but thousands of these various copies remain. Some of the copies are torn and have text missing; some have errors and typos; and some have the notes people made accidentally integrated into the text. However, many of the copies have the text intact, just the way you wrote it.

Could a person study all these copies and *reasonably* determine what you actually said? The answer is yes, and this is the same kind of thing that happened with the Gospels.

More than 2,000 manuscripts and manuscript fragments exist from the earliest centuries of the church, and these represent every portion of the Gospels. More than 90% of the Gospels is fully recoverable, and more than 50% is free of textual variants (those typos, paraphrases, misspellings, etc.).

For those manuscripts that have textual variants, a comparison is enough to determine the original content. For example, consider the following sentences, taken from five different fragments of a document:

- The **brown** *cat* ran into the **blue** house.
- The **brwn** caterpillar ran into the **blue** house
- The orange *cat* walked into the **blue** house.
- The **brown** *cat* ran into the bleu hut.

- The **brown** *cat* <u>ran</u> into the red <u>house</u>.

So in evaluating these fragments, we must ask the following questions: was the subject a cat or a caterpillar, was it brown or orange, did it walk or run, did they go into a house or a hut, and was that structure red or blue?

The overwhelming evidence indicates a brown cat ran into a blue house. Only one of the fragments says caterpillar; only one says the cat was red; only one says the structure was a hut; and only one says the structure was red. In the same way, because of the overwhelming agreement between the Gospel fragments and copies, we can be certain that the Gospels we have represent what the original authors actually said.

2. WHY DO THE GOSPELS TELL DIFFERENT STORIES ABOUT JESUS?

The Gospels are a combination of eyewitness accounts, storytelling, and research conducted. And there's a lot to tell over the course of even three years of a person's life, as was likely the timeframe covered in the Gospels.

If you were writing about a three-year period in your life, would you include every little detail? First, you couldn't because the book would be way too long. Second, even if you *could* record everything, you shouldn't, because the book would then be too boring. Instead, you would pick out the highlights, just enough to tell people what you want them to know and make them feel how you want them to feel.

The Gospel writers recorded the various details and aspects of Jesus' life that they witnessed and felt were significant. In the case of Luke's Gospel, he tells us upfront that he has done his research on the events he writes about (Luke 1:1-4). However, the important events of Jesus' life are recorded by most, if not all, of the Gospel writers.

This is similar to what would happen with any major news event today. There isn't much value in four accounts that are exactly the same, right? If you consult four different news outlets for details on a story, you're seeking new information with each one, not the same thing every other source has. We gain more value from different viewpoints and varied details. This gives us a well-rounded picture of what took place.

Only two of the Gospels were written by one of the 12 apostles—those who lived in daily communion with Jesus. Those two were Matthew and John, and of the two, only one was part of Jesus' inner circle—the Apostle John. Both Luke and Mark were companions of the Apostle Paul, so they didn't hang out with the 12 apostles.

Because of the differences in the individual writers' relationship with Jesus, we'd naturally expect different details due to the perspective of each writer. Note, for example, how John's Gospel often provides more intimate details than Matthew's or Mark's Gospel.

3. WHO WROTE THE FOUR GOSPELS?

The Gospels are most commonly attributed to the people who bear the names of each book—Matthew, Mark, Luke, and John. The early church fathers, which include Papias and Irenaeus, identified the author of each Gospel in their writings, giving us further confidence that the person named as the writer is the person who wrote it. They lived close to the events of the Gospels and therefore knew firsthand who wrote them.

4. WHO WAS THE GOSPEL WRITER MATTHEW?

Matthew, also known as Levi (Mark 2:14; Luke 5:27–28), was the writer of the first Gospel and was one of the 12 apostles. He was unpopular and an outcast because he was a tax collector (Matthew 9:9). But Jesus still called him to follow him and become his disciple. Tradition states that "Matthew put forth a Gospel writing among the Hebrews in their own speech while Peter and Paul were preaching the Gospel in Rome and founding the church there."

5. WHO WAS THE GOSPEL WRITER MARK?

Mark was the writer of the second Gospel; his full name was John Mark. He was not an apostle but was a companion of Paul and Barnabas and a friend/follower of the apostle Peter (Acts 12:25). According to Papias, one of the early bishops of the second century, "Mark, the interpreter of Peter, wrote down accurately all the words or deeds of the Lord of which he [Peter] made mention, but not in order…"

Here's a fun fact: Mark is often identified as the young man in Mark 14:51 who was present when Jesus was arrested. The soldiers seized this young man but he escaped, leaving his clothing behind and running away naked.

And identifying him as John Mark does make sense. First, it's an odd detail to include randomly unless the young man in question was significant in some way. Second, it's a very specific detail, something only the person who experienced it firsthand would likely record.

The fact that the writer doesn't directly identify himself or speak in the first person mirrors the way the other Gospel writers wrote. Matthew didn't identify himself when he discussed Jesus calling him from a life of tax collecting, and the Apostle John didn't identify himself in the numerous events he was a part of. Modest, these fellas!

6. WHO WAS THE GOSPEL WRITER LUKE?

Luke was the writer of the third Gospel. He was not an apostle but a Gentile (meaning not Jewish) physician and a friend of the

Apostle Paul (Colossians 4:11-14). He likely had close contact with Mary since he wrote in so much detail about Jesus' early life that only a family member would know.

Tradition states that "Luke, the companion of Paul, set down in a book the Gospel proclaimed by that apostle." Luke is also the author of Acts, which can be considered a sequel to the book that bears his name. Now, movie sequels often get a bad rap, but the sequel to the book of Luke is pretty good!

7. WHO WAS THE GOSPEL WRITER JOHN?

John wrote the fourth Gospel and was one of the 12 apostles—he is not to be confused with John the Baptist or John Mark. The Apostle John refers to himself in his own Gospel as *the disciple Jesus loved* (John 13:23). He had a brother named James, who was also one of the 12 apostles (Mark 3:17).

The mother of James and John was Salome, one of the women who was near the cross when Jesus was crucified and who visited the tomb early that Sunday morning (Mark 16:1). She was likely Mary's (Jesus' mother) sister (John 19:25; Mark 15:40), so the Apostle John was probably Jesus' first cousin.

Many passages support John being related to Jesus:

- **Jesus entrusted his mother to John** (John 19:26-27): It makes sense that Jesus would place his mother in the care of a relative.
- **The High Priest knew him** (John 18:15-16): John the Baptist's father, Zechariah, was a priest. And John the Baptist was related to Jesus (Luke 1:36; Luke 1:57-60) and, by association, the Apostle John. Since they were all family, John was probably well-connected with the priestly family.
- John was part of the inner circle of disciples (Luke 8:51; Luke 9:28)
- John (and his brother) requested (through his mother Salome) to sit on each side of Jesus in his kingdom (Matthew 20:20-21). This request makes sense if they felt special because of their kinship to Jesus.

Tradition states that "John, the disciple of the Lord, who reclined on his bosom, in turn published his Gospel while he was staying in Ephesus in Asia." John also wrote the three New Testament letters—First, Second, and Third John—as well as the book of Revelation.

8. WHO IS THE "DISCIPLE JESUS LOVED" REFERRED TO IN JOHN'S GOSPEL?

Several times in the Gospel of John, the writer refers to "the disciple Jesus loved" (John 21:20-23; 13:23; 20:2; 21:7; 21:20). The consensus is that the writer is referring to himself. We already discussed that the writer was the Apostle John, as well as the modesty of the apostles when writing about themselves.

He is *never* mentioned by name in the Gospel of John, but we know from the other Gospels that he was present at key events. Since he is the only one not mentioned by name in the Gospel of John, he must be the disciple Jesus loved. (The references to "John" in this Gospel primarily refer to John the Baptist, with a couple of the references referring to Simon Peter's father).

Also, I like to think he identifies himself this way with a sense of awe rather than an attitude of superiority. Like, "Wow, Jesus really loved me."

9. WHY IS JOHN THE ONLY WRITER TO RECORD LAZARUS' RESURRECTION?

It's a fair question. Of all of Jesus' miracles, raising someone from the dead is definitely the biggest. We simply don't know why the Apostle John is the only Gospel writer to record Lazarus' resurrection.

However, it's important to note that there were other resurrections that were also not recorded by all the Gospel writers. These are all of Jesus' resurrection miracles:

- The raising of a widow's son: Luke 7:11-17
- The raising of Jairus' daughter: Luke 8:41-56, Matthew 9:18-26, Mark 5:22-43
- The raising of Lazarus: John chapter 11

Only Luke records the raising of the widow's son, and only John records the raising of Lazarus. Now yes, Lazarus' resurrection was unique compared to the others. In the other two cases, Jesus raised them soon after they died, but in Lazarus' case, he waited three days. The Jews acknowledged that someone was truly dead only after three days had passed. So when Jesus raised Lazarus to life, no one could say he wasn't really dead, that he was merely in a coma. (Incidentally, this may be the reason why Jesus rose on the third day.)

One explanation for three of the Gospel writers not including the resurrection of Lazarus is that it was probably the most public of Jesus' resurrection miracles. He did it near Jerusalem, which was enemy territory. He did it in front of a crowd of people, which also included the Jews, who went and told the Jewish leaders what had happened.

This news ultimately led to their decision to have Jesus killed. Since everyone was talking about the incident, some of the Gospel writers might have felt it wasn't necessary to include it. But John wanted to bring out a certain theological significance, so he included it. However, we can really only speculate about why each writer included or left out the things they did.

CHAPTER TWO

EARLY YEARS

10. WHEN WAS JESUS BORN?

The Gospels don't give us a specific date; however, they do provide significant events that help us determine the approximate time frame. To arrive at a possible date for Jesus' birth of around March of 4 B.C., scholars have calculated the dates of several events mentioned in the Gospels—Herod's reign and death (Matthew 2:1; Matthew 2:15), the reigns of Caesar Augustus and Quirinius' (Luke 2:1-2), and the reigns of Tiberius Caesar and Pontius Pilate (Luke 3:1).

We don't know the exact date of Jesus' birth, and it's not that important (*I know. It feels important, but it's really not.*) We can celebrate Jesus' birth anytime, and we have chosen to do so on December 25. This issue causes too much strife among believers, and we must stop arguing about such insignificant matters. Don't worry, we'll talk more about Christmas later.

11. WHY IS JESUS' BIRTH IN BETHLEHEM SIGNIFICANT?

The city of Bethlehem was a small and insignificant village until it grew prominent due to the significant events that took place there. Bethlehem was located about five miles south of Jerusalem. Here are some of the events that took place there:

- A. Rachel gave birth to Joseph's younger brother Benjamin and died there.
- B. Naomi and Ruth settled there.
- C. Ruth and Boaz started a family there, making it the birthplace of their great-grandson, David.

Bethlehem is often called the city of David. Jesus was born there because his stepfather Joseph was of the house and lineage of David (Luke 2:4), and he had to go to Bethlehem to be registered for the census. This fulfilled the prophecy about the Messiah and his birthplace (Micah 5:2; Matthew 2:4-6).

12. WAS JESUS REALLY BORN IN A MANGER/STABLE?

Jesus was certainly born in a manger, as stated in Luke 2:7. However, the question is whether he was actually born in a barn or stable. It may not have been a stable as we know it today. When people stopped for the night at an inn or at someone's house, they needed a place to store their animals. Therefore, quarters attached to the buildings were set aside for their animals. Jesus was likely born in such a structure.

13. WHY WAS THERE NO ROOM AT THE INN FOR MARY AND JOSEPH?

Because of the census required by Caesar Augustus, many people had gone to Bethlehem to be registered (Luke chapter 2). Sometimes this story is told as if evil people owned the inn and just turned Jesus and his parents away for no reason. But in reality, with so many people traveling to Bethlehem and looking for a place to stay, the inns simply ran out of room. This is similar to what would happen if there was a big convention or concert in New York City; most hotels would be booked.

14. WAS JESUS CIRCUMCISED?

Yes, Jesus was a Jew, and so he was circumcised. Mary and Joseph were obedient and followed the requirements of the law. According to Luke 2:21, Jesus was circumcised on the eighth day after he was born, the same day he was officially named.

15. WHY WASN'T JESUS CALLED IMMANUEL IN ACCORDANCE WITH ISAIAH 7:14 AND MATTHEW 1:23?

Although Immanuel is a common name today, it served as a title for Jesus, not the name he would be referred to in his daily life. Isaiah prophesied about the Messiah, saying, *His name shall be called Wonderful Counselor, Mighty God, Everlasting Father, Prince of Peace* (Isaiah 9:6). These, like Immanuel, are all titles and descriptions of Jesus rather than actual names.

Matthew tells us that this title means "God with us."

16. WHY ARE MATTHEW'S AND LUKE'S GENEALOGIES FOR JESUS SO DIFFERENT?

Genealogies are very prominent in the Bible, as they reveal a person's ancestry and lineage. In Jesus' case, his lineage was particularly important in demonstrating that he was the one all the prophets had written about. For this reason, both Matthew and Luke included it (Matthew 1:1-17, Luke 3:1-38).

However, the two genealogies can be quite confusing because they both appear to be through Joseph's line, though they consist of different names. Matthew says Joseph's father was Jacob, and Luke appears to say Joseph's father was Heli. The difficulty can be resolved if Matthew traces Jesus' genealogy through his adoptive father Joseph and Luke traces Jesus' genealogy through Mary, specifically through her father Heli (who would have been Joseph's father-in-law).

Despite the wording, I don't believe Luke intends to identify Heli as Joseph's father. The passage begins by making the point that Jesus was "thought to be the son of Joseph." So it clearly wants us to know that

Jesus isn't Joseph's biological son. After this statement, the genealogy continues.

I believe the mention of Joseph is more of an aside and he's not actually being included in the genealogy. Accepting this premise, the passage would read as follows: "Now Jesus was thought to be the son of Joseph. **He** was the son of Heli, the son of………"

So the "**he**" in the second sentence would refer to Jesus, not Joseph. This is the stance adopted in *Behold the Lamb ~ A Harmony of the Gospels* (The Chronological Word Truth Life Bible).

Now, people in those days often did have two names, and it's possible that Jacob and Heli were the same person. However, this is unlikely. Remember that Jesus is called the seed of David. Now, he could still be considered of the line of David legally due to being adopted by Joseph. But to be called his seed indicates a physical connection, and Jesus only had that connection through Mary.

Another supporting factor that Luke recorded Jesus' genealogy through Mary is that women often married within their tribe. For example, we see that her relative Elizabeth married Zechariah, and they were both descendants of Aaron, who was from the tribe of Levi (Luke 1:5).

While we may never completely understand the differences between the two genealogies, one thing for certain is that they both demonstrate that Jesus was from the line of David and, therefore, could rightfully be called King and Messiah.

17. WHO WAS HEROD?

When we consider Herod, we think of the king who reigned when Jesus was born. However, most people don't realize that many different Herods are mentioned in the Bible. So when reading the Gospels in particular, you'll want to identify which Herod the writer is referring to.

THE HERODS	DESCRIPTION	SCRIPTURE
Herod the Great	Governor of Galilee who ordered all the male children killed	Matthew 2:16
Herod Archelaus	Herod the Great's son, who ruled Judea after his death	Matthew 2:21-22
Herod Antipas	Archelaus' younger brother, who ruled Galilee and Perea. He beheaded John the Baptist for scolding him for sleeping with his brother's wife. Also, Pilate sent Jesus to him after finding him guilty of no crime.	Matthew 14:3-12 Luke 23:6-12

THE HERODS	DESCRIPTION	SCRIPTURE
Philip the Tetrarch (or Herod Philip)	Son of Herod the Great and Cleopatra, who ruled Iturea and Traconitis. He lost his wife, Herodias, to his brother Herod Antipas.	Matthew 14:3-12 Luke 3:1
Herod Agrippa I	Herodias' brother, who killed the Apostle James and put Peter in prison.	Acts 12:1-19
Herod Agrippa II	Asked by Festus to hear Paul's case; he found no fault in Paul but refused to be converted to Christianity.	Acts 25:13 – 26:31

So Herod the Great was King when Jesus was born, and he was the one who tried to have all the infant boys killed. He died shortly after Jesus' birth. The next prominent Herod in the Gospels is Herod Antipas. He was the one who beheaded John the Baptist and the one Pilate sent Jesus to when he heard Jesus was a Galilean.

Considering so many Herods, it's likely to assume it was more of a title than a name.

18. WHY DID HEROD THE GREAT WANT JESUS KILLED AS A BABY?

Herod wanted the infant Jesus killed because he felt threatened. He believed in the prophecy of one who would be born King of the Jews. Taking this literally, he thought the child would take over his throne; therefore, he decided to have him killed (Matthew 2:1-3).

19. DID MARY REMAIN A VIRGIN AFTER GIVING BIRTH TO JESUS?

Contrary to certain teachings, Mary did not remain a virgin after giving birth to Jesus. She and Joseph abstained from sex only until Jesus was born (Matthew 1:24-25). After that, they had a normal marital relationship and had sons and daughters together (Mark 6:3).

20. IS IT IMPORTANT TO BELIEVE THAT JESUS WAS BORN OF A VIRGIN?

The virgin birth of Christ is one of the central teachings of Christianity. The way Jesus came into this world is important because it was necessary for him to be born without a sinful human nature. The angel explains to Mary that Jesus will be conceived by the Holy Spirit (Luke 1:35; Matthew 1:20).

Therefore, Mary had nothing to do with Jesus' conception; she was only the vessel — a surrogate carrying someone else's baby. Without the virgin birth, Jesus is just a man no different from any other. And if that were the case, he wouldn't be able to save us.

21. WHY IS JESUS' CHILDHOOD NOT RECORDED?

Most of Jesus' childhood isn't recorded because the disciples shared only the information they felt pertinent to Jesus' mission and ministry on earth. His birth was important, as was his time in the synagogue discussing God with the Jewish leaders at the age of 12. Aside from those things, he probably had an average childhood, so the Gospel writers felt no need to elaborate on it.

22. DID JESUS HAVE SIBLINGS?

Yes, Jesus had brothers as well as unnamed sisters. His brothers' names were James, Joseph, Simon, and Judas (Matthew 13:55-56). These are not the same men as the apostles of the same name. Initially, none of his siblings believed in him.

However, two of them do play prominent roles later in the Bible. His brother Judas wrote the book of Jude in the New Testament. And his brother James wrote the book of James. He also became the leader of the church in Jerusalem after Jesus' death and was instrumental in the development of the early church.

23. WHO WAS JOHN THE BAPTIST?

John the Baptist was probably called "the Baptist" to distinguish him from the Apostle John. His parents were Zechariah and Elizabeth, and Elizabeth was related to Jesus' mother Mary (Luke 1:21, 24; Luke 1:36). Therefore, John the Baptist was probably Jesus' second or third cousin Elizabeth and Mary probably weren't sisters, because the Bible likely would have just said so. They were probably cousins, or Elizabeth could have been Mary's aunt. All we really know for sure is that he was related to Jesus in some way.

John the Baptist was important because he bridged the prophetic gap between the Old and the New Testament. In other words, there were no prophets for over 400 years when John the Baptist suddenly arrived preaching about repentance ... and a Messiah.

We first meet John when he jumped for joy in Elizabeth's womb when a pregnant Mary visited her (Luke 1:41). Later, as a somewhat odd man, he goes to live in the desert and begins preaching a baptism of repentance. He was the voice "calling out in the wilderness" and "preparing the way for the Lord (Isaiah 40:3 and Malachi 3:1).

Jesus goes to John to be baptized, leading the way for his believers to do the same. Later, John is put in prison and then beheaded for his righteous teachings against Herod's infidelity. His time on earth was short, but wow, what a calling he had!

CHAPTER THREE

DAILY LIFE

24. WHY WAS JESUS BAPTIZED?

Jesus' request to be baptized was so odd that even John the Baptist questioned him. He understood that Jesus was superior to him and that it should be the other way around. John was baptizing people for the repentance of their sins, and he knew Jesus had no need to repent.

However, Jesus insisted, but why? He tells us himself. He says this act will "fulfill all righteousness" (Matthew 3:13-15), but what does that mean? Jesus doesn't elaborate. However, God gave both visual and verbal approval after Jesus was baptized, making it clear that Jesus was certainly doing his Father's will (Matthew 3:16-17).

Jesus' baptism seems to be an early indication of his humility, of the way he "emptied himself," as discussed in Philippians 2:5-11. Here are some possible reasons why Jesus was baptized:

- To serve as an example to his followers to do likewise.
- To identify with his followers. Scripture states that Jesus can identify with us because (1) He was tempted just as we are (Hebrews 2:18) and (2) He became sin for us (2 Corinthians 5:21). So it makes sense that he chose to identify with us in baptism as well.
- To demonstrate that he had given himself over fully to God. Baptism isn't only for the person undergoing the process; it's also for those witnessing it. It's a statement to God, to ourselves, and to others that we have dedicated ourselves to following his teachings.

25. DID ONLY ONE WOMAN ANOINT JESUS' FEET OR WAS IT TWO DIFFERENT WOMEN?

In the Gospels, there are two similar stories about a woman who anointed Jesus' feet. One occurs early in Jesus' ministry (Luke 7:36-50), and the other occurs just before his death (Matthew 26:6-13).

Matthew 26:6-13 is the same event found in Mark 14:3-9 and John 12:1-8. It's clear that these three passages refer to the same event because they agree that it takes place in Bethany. Matthew and Mark also both agree the dinner was hosted by Simon the Leper.

All three also contain a discussion by the disciples regarding the woman's "waste" of expensive perfume. Jesus rebukes them and states that she is preparing his body for his burial. John identifies the woman who anointed Jesus as Mary, the sister of Martha and Lazarus.

In contrast, we have the passage in Luke 7:36-50. Again, we have a man named Simon hosting a dinner, and again, we have a woman anointing Jesus. However, this time, Simon is not a leper, but a Pharisee, and there is no indication of who the woman is.

And instead of the disciples complaining that she was wasting money, the Pharisee complains that she is a sinner. Also, if this woman was Mary of Bethany, Luke probably would have identified her as such. But he doesn't mention Mary of Bethany by name until Luke 10:39-42, and he introduces this unnamed woman as if this is the first time he's talking about her.

Therefore, it's wise to conclude that two different women anointed Jesus. While there are similarities between the two events, they aren't significant. Simon was a common name, and anointing a religious leader with perfume was probably common during that time, similar to the way we naturally offer someone a drink when they visit us.

26. WHY DID JESUS WRITE IN THE DIRT WHEN THE ADULTEROUS WOMAN WAS BROUGHT TO HIM?

In John 8:6-11, the Jewish leaders brought to Jesus a woman they had caught committing adultery. Several times during the encounter, Jesus kneeled and wrote on the ground. Unfortunately, we can only speculate about why Jesus did this and what he wrote because Scripture doesn't tell us.

I believe Jesus was possibly disengaging himself from the Jewish leaders, refusing to be baited into their trap. The scriptures say they kept on questioning him, but he spent most of the time they were there writing on the ground.

It doesn't seem like they could see what he was writing, or if they did, it had no significance for them. They only react when Jesus speaks to them, when he says the person without sin should be the first to throw a stone.

27. HOW LONG WAS JESUS' MINISTRY ON EARTH?

According to John's Gospel, Jesus attended at least three annual Passover Feasts throughout the course of his ministry (John 2:13; John 6:4; and John 11:55–57). Based on that information alone, Jesus' ministry would have been between two and three years.

Scholars also believe there was another Passover not mentioned by the Gospel writers. By the time of that first Passover (in the spring of 27), Jesus had already conducted a ministry that would have taken several months. Finally, there is the 40-day period between Jesus' resurrection and ascension (Acts 1:3). Considering all this information, Jesus' ministry likely lasted 3½ years.

28. WHY DIDN'T JESUS STAY ON EARTH LONGER?

While Jesus was on earth for about 33 years, his public ministry lasted only about 3 years. Jesus' disciples clearly would have been thrilled to have Jesus remain with them a little longer, so why didn't he?

It seems Jesus stayed only long enough to accomplish his mission on earth. After selecting his disciples, who would carry on his work, preaching the Word to Israel, and offering himself as the ultimate sacrifice, his work was done. So it was time to ascend to heaven to reclaim his rightful place at his Father's side.

Also, Jesus himself stated that if he didn't leave, the Holy Spirit couldn't come (John 16: 7). While Jesus on earth was powerful, he was limited because, in his humanity, he could only be in one place at a time. However, the Holy Spirit would dwell within each believer and spread his power throughout the world.

29. DID JESUS HAVE A SENSE OF HUMOR?

The average depiction of Jesus portrays quite a serious demeanor, making it seem that Jesus never cracked a smile. However, common sense tells us that Jesus was a normal human being and, as such, he experienced all the emotions we do. This includes both joy and laughter.

Additionally, Jesus' teachings indicate that he had a sense of humor. Take some time to really visualize a log sticking out of someone's eye (Matthew 7:3-5)! Who comes up with something like that without a sense of humor?

30. WHY IS JESUS OFTEN REFERRED TO AS JESUS OF NAZARETH?

Jesus was probably called Jesus of Nazareth primarily to differentiate him from others of the same name. In biblical times, people were often referred to by their place of residence to distinguish them from those who had the same first name. So we have Mary of Magdala (Mary Magdalene), Simon of Cyrene, and Joseph of Arimathea. Although Jesus was born in Bethlehem, he was raised in Nazareth (Matthew 2:23), so that's how people identified him.

31. WHAT LANGUAGE DID JESUS SPEAK?

Jesus likely primarily spoke Aramaic, as it was the common language in Judea and Galilee. He probably also spoke some Greek and Hebrew. *Talitha koum* (Mark 5:41); *ephphatha* (Mark 7:34); *eloi eloi lama sabachthani* (Matthew 27:46, Mark 15:34); and *abba* (Mark 14:36) are all Aramaic words spoken by Jesus.

32. WAS JESUS MARRIED?

No. Nothing in the Bible indicates that Jesus was married. This idea comes from fictional accounts of his life, such as the *Da Vinci Code*. There would have been nothing inherently wrong if Jesus had been married. However, it's unlikely that the Bible would fail to mention a wife if she existed. Also, because of Jesus' earthly mission, there would have been no purpose for a wife. Jesus came to give his life for the sins of mankind, not start a family.

33. WHY WAS JESUS ANGRY WITH THE MERCHANTS IN THE TEMPLE?

When people went to Jerusalem for Passover, they often needed to exchange their Roman coins for a Jewish half-shekel to purchase the required animals to make their sacrifices. So the moneychangers and merchants were likely abusing a legitimate practice by charging high fees and cheating the people. This is indicated in Matthew 21:13 when Jesus says they are making God's house a den of thieves.

34. HOW MANY TIMES DID JESUS CLEANSE THE TEMPLE?

Jesus cleansed the temple twice. The first time was early in his ministry (John 2:13-17). The second time was a few days before his crucifixion (Matthew 21:12-13). Both times, he angered the Jewish leaders, demonstrating the kind of authority they had never seen before. Jesus frequently traveled to Jerusalem, so he had many chances to confront the merchants in the temple. And he probably did so every time!

35. WHERE WAS JOSEPH DURING JESUS' MINISTRY?

Mary's husband Joseph seems to disappear from the Gospel narratives early on. We don't hear any more about him after he moves his family from Egypt and settles in Nazareth. The consensus is that he must have been a lot older than Mary and probably died before Jesus began his ministry. Jesus didn't begin his ministry until he was about 30 years old, so it's not farfetched that Joseph died within that time if he wasn't a young man when Jesus was born.

36. WHAT DID JESUS LOOK LIKE?

The closest thing we have to a physical description of Jesus is in Isaiah 53:2b: *He had no beauty or majesty to attract us to him, nothing in his appearance that we should desire him.* Isaiah 52:14 tells us that during Jesus' crucifixion, he was so disfigured that he was barely recognized as a human. These descriptions really don't tell us much.

Revelation 1:14-15 describes him this way: his hair white like wool, eyes of blazing fire, and feet like bronze. This passage is often used to prove that Jesus was a black man.

However, this scripture is not trying to give us a physical description.

If we interpret this part literally, as a physical description, we'd have to interpret the next verses literally too and conclude that *his voice sounded like rushing waters, he held seven stars in his right hand, and there was a sword coming out of his mouth*. But no one believes Jesus was walking around with a sword hanging from his mouth.

Because Jesus was Jewish, many of the images we have of him today are not accurate. He obviously wasn't blond-haired and blue-eyed, but this doesn't mean he was black either. Many of the features used to describe black people could also be used to describe Jews, who had dark skin, dark eyes, and dark hair.

37. WHO ARE ALL THE MARYS IN THE GOSPELS?

Mary is one of the most common names in biblical times, so it's no surprise that we find multiple Marys in the Gospels. They are:

- **Mary the mother of Jesus** (Matthew 1:16): She was married to Joseph and had a relative named Elizabeth and a sister named Salome. Her nephews were the apostles James and John.

- **Mary Magdalene** (Mark 16:9): Jesus had healed her by casting several demons out of her. She followed him with a group of other women during his travels, and she was the first person Jesus appeared to after his resurrection. She is also the one who told his disciples he was alive.

- **Mary the wife of Clopas** (Mark 15:40; John 19:25): She had two sons named Joseph and James (These men are not the same as Jesus' brothers, his father, or the disciples of the same name). This Mary was also one of the women who visited Jesus' tomb with Mary Magdalene.

- **Mary of Bethany** (John 11:1,18): She lived in Bethany, which was not far from Jerusalem. She had a sister named Martha and a brother named Lazarus, who Jesus raised from the dead. She also anointed Jesus before his death (John 12:1-3) and made

Martha mad because she was listening to him teach while Martha was doing all the work (Luke 10:38-42).

38. WHY DID JESUS CURSE THE FIG TREE?

Just days before his crucifixion, Jesus curses a fig tree, an action which some find confusing and perhaps a little unfair to the tree. Jesus comes upon a fig tree, and scripture says it wasn't the season for figs. But when Jesus found no fruit, he cursed the tree (Mark 11:12-14).

This is the only miracle of destruction that we find Jesus performing, and it seems out of character, so it bears some explaining.

The best explanation is that Jesus, rather than just telling a parable, acted out a parable for dramatic effect. In the Old Testament, God had a few prophets do something similar, Hosea for example:

> When the LORD first spoke to Hosea, He said this to him: "Go and marry a promiscuous wife and have children of promiscuity, for the land is committing blatant acts

> of promiscuity by abandoning the LORD."
>
> So he went and married Gomer daughter of Diblaim, and she conceived and bore him a son. (Hosea 1:1-3a)

So Jesus wasn't mad at the fig tree but just making a visual point. Like Israel, this fig tree was barren and wasn't producing fruit. It's likely an allusion to Jeremiah 8:13:

> "I would have gathered their harvest," declares the LORD, "but there are no grapes on the vine. There are no figs on the tree, and the leaves have dried up. What I have given them will be taken away."

Like the tree, Israel was not producing fruit; therefore, the nation would no longer be the primary vehicle through whom God would accomplish his purpose. We see this in action through Paul's ministry, when he turns his attention from the Jews to the Gentiles. As he always did, God would eventually redeem them, but they had to endure many lessons first.

39. WHAT WAS THE TRANSFIGURATION AND WHY WAS IT SIGNIFICANT?

The transfiguration was an event that took place on a mountain about a week after Peter confessed Jesus as the Christ at Caesarea Philippi (Matthew 17:1–8; Mark 9:2–8; Luke 9:28–36). While Jesus was on the mountain with his apostles Peter, James, and John, his appearance suddenly changed. His face shone like the sun and his clothes turned a dazzling white. Moses and Elijah appeared dressed in splendor and spoke with Jesus about his impending death.

When Peter saw this, he offered to make tents for them all, but God's voice interrupted and identified Jesus as his Son, admonishing the disciples to listen to him. For the disciples, seeing Jesus in his glorious splendor talking with the prophets of old was confirmation of what Peter had just stated at Caesarea: that Jesus was the Christ, the son of the living God.

CHAPTER FOUR

TEACHINGS AND DOCTRINE

40. DID JESUS TEACH THAT WE SHOULDN'T JUDGE?

One of the most popular scriptures quoted by both Christians and non-Christians is the first part of Matthew 7:1: *Judge not*. The rest of the verse, and even the whole passage, is conveniently left out. As a result, many believers spread the teaching that we should never judge. But they have missed the meaning of Jesus' words. Jesus didn't teach that we shouldn't judge but that if we do judge, we should do so without hypocrisy. In other words, don't judge someone if you are guilty of the same or a worse sin.

The full text reads as follows:

"Do not judge, or you too will be judged. For in the same way you judge others, you will be judged, and with the measure you use, it will be measured to you.

"Why do you look at the speck of sawdust in your brother's eye and pay no attention to the plank in your own eye? How can you say to your brother, 'Let me take the speck out of your eye,' when all the time there is a plank in your own eye? You hypocrite, first take the plank out of your own eye, and then you will see clearly to remove the speck from your brother's eye (Matthew 7:1-5).

Jesus said *first* take the plank out of your own eye and then you can see clearly enough to remove the sawdust from your brother's eye. But today's teaching would have us believe that even acknowledging the sawdust is wrong, because that would be "judging." But how can we help someone remove what we refuse to see?

Now, it's true that we should avoid judging someone's heart and avoid condemning anyone. Only God knows a person's heart, and they may be working things out behind the scenes, where our human eyes can't yet see the fruit. But 9 times out of 10, when people say don't judge, they simply mean, don't call my sin a sin. And that's just completely unbiblical.

It goes against the teachings of Jesus in Matthew 18:15-17:

> If your brother or sister sins, go and point out their fault, just between the two of you. If they listen to you, you have won them over.

It also goes against the teachings of the rest of the Bible. Consider this scripture from the apostle Paul:

> "Brothers and sisters, if someone is caught in a sin, you who live by the Spirit should restore that person gently. But watch yourselves, or you also may be tempted" (Galatians 6:1).

How can we restore anyone if we can't even identify what they're doing as sin?

The teaching that we shouldn't judge is a very dangerous one. It causes us to ignore sin, and even to embrace it. We don't want to be accused of judging, and so we go to great lengths to avoid doing so. But listen, it's totally ok to judge sin. Don't judge the person, but do call a spade a spade. You can't help someone put out a fire if you're not allowed to acknowledge that there *is* a fire.

This false teaching makes us silent about sin when we really need to be exposing it, speaking out against it, and restoring those who are trapped in it to a relationship with Jesus Christ.

41. WHAT IS BLASPHEMY AGAINST THE HOLY SPIRIT?

In Matthew 12:31, Jesus makes this striking statement: *And so I tell you, every kind of sin and slander can be forgiven, but blasphemy against the Spirit will not be forgiven.* The subject of the unforgivable sin is hotly debated among Christians, and it is even a source of concern for those who wonder if they've been guilty of committing it.

The first thing to do when confronted with a difficult scripture is to read the entire passage in which it is found. So for this topic, we really need to read Matthew 12:22-37.

What's the context in which Jesus is speaking? Well, it's another encounter with the Jewish leaders. Jesus has just cast out a demon, and the Pharisees say he can only cast out demons because he is possessed by a demon. Specifically, they're saying the power he has is given to him by the chief of demons (Beelzebub/Satan). They attribute Jesus' healing of the demon-possessed man to Satan instead of the Holy Spirit.

It was in direct response to this statement that Jesus spoke these words about blasphemy. He said they would be forgiven for speaking against him (the Son of Man), but they wouldn't be forgiven for speaking against the Holy Spirit.

You see, it was possible for the Pharisees not to fully understand who Jesus was, but after all they had seen, they had no reason to deny God's Spirit that was clearly at work through him.

One might be temporarily confused about Jesus and speak against him or rebuke him. Just think about Peter's denial of Jesus (Matthew 26:69-75) or even his statement that Jesus must not be crucified (Matthew 26:21-23). Yet we know Peter was forgiven and restored. These things came from not fully understanding Jesus and also from human weakness (Indeed, none of the disciples fully understood Jesus and his mission until after he had been raised from the dead, and initially, they didn't even believe he was alive.) So we can see the difference between momentary confusion/weakness and a willful disregard of the Spirit at work.

But the Pharisees weren't just confused; the words they spoke revealed the true state of their hearts. For all their knowledge of the Old Testament, they weren't true believers. They didn't *want* to believe! My personal theory is that a true believer can't commit blasphemy against the Holy Spirit. So if you're worried that you've committed this sin, it's a good indication that you haven't.

42. AREN'T CHRISTMAS AND EASTER PAGAN HOLIDAYS?

No, Christmas and Easter aren't pagan holidays, but they were created to replace pagan holidays. However, some of the elements of the original holiday remained, which is why we have things like the Easter bunny and Santa. Some make the case that it's wrong to celebrate these holidays because they contain elements that have nothing to do with Jesus. I disagree. Those of us who celebrate Easter and Christmas know who and what we're celebrating.

The Apostle Paul had a lot to say about the subject. He preached against those who judge others regarding holidays (and other silly stuff). For more on the subject, I'll include an expanded version of a blog post I wrote.

****

AWAY WITH THE MANGER: FREQUENTLY ASKED QUESTIONS ABOUT CHRISTIANS AND CHRISTMAS

Every year around Christmas, social media is slammed with posts about how Christmas is a pagan holiday. Not only that, but they helpfully explain that Jesus wasn't born on December 25th. Is there any truth to these claims, and does it matter? Should Christians stay away from this holiday because of its so-called pagan origins? I'll answer those questions and more in this article.

Should Christians celebrate Christmas? Sure. It's an awesome holiday. Jesus, Gifts, Family, Food, Holiday Cheer....what's not to like? On a serious note, this is a flawed question. There's no "should" or "shouldn't." Contrary to what some would have us believe, this isn't a moral issue; it's a preference issue, but we'll get to that a little later.

But isn't Christmas a pagan holiday? Only if you're a pagan! A day is just a day, and it is whatever you make it. As stated earlier, Christmas didn't originate as a pagan holiday; it merely coincided with pagan holidays.

What does pagan mean, anyway? Generally, it means one who worships other 'gods.' It can also refer to someone who is ungodly. For Christians, this means anyone who doesn't worship the one true God, as revealed in the Bible.

Doesn't Jeremiah 10:1-5 prohibit Christmas trees in: Nope, not at all. At that time, there was no such thing as Christmas or Christmas trees. This scripture merely prohibits the creating and worshiping of idols. Go on and read it for yourself.

In those days, they made idols from the wood of trees. They cut a tree down, overlaid it with silver and gold, and called it their god. God concludes in this passage that their idols are like scarecrows: they can't speak and they can't walk.

A Christmas tree is just an object; it's not inherently good or bad. If you're calling the tree your god and bowing down in worship to it, then you've got bigger problems than we're discussing here. But if not, decorate your tree and enjoy it to your heart's content.

Didn't Christ instruct us to remember his death, not his birth? He did instruct us to remember his death, but he never said we couldn't celebrate his birth. We can't make an argument against something based solely on lack of instruction. The Bible is silent on many of our contemporary activities simply because they didn't exist back then.

When we acknowledge Jesus' birth, we do so in anticipation of his death. Christmas isn't so much about the baby in the manger as much as it is about the Christ on the cross. He was born to die for our sins, and THAT'S the cause for celebration.

Christmas has become so commercialized; shouldn't we avoid contributing to the madness? Yes, you should. Fortunately, you can celebrate AND avoid contributing to the madness. Don't condemn something good because of others' abuse of it. Keep Christ at the center, give gifts, and have fun.

Isn't it a shame that so many people go into debt for Christmas? Yes it is, so limit or avoid debt. Spend what you can afford. We should manage our money wisely at any time of the year. The Bible instructs us to be good stewards over our possessions, so this applies even at Christmas.

But don't you know that Jesus wasn't really born on December 25? Yes, yes, a thousand times yes. Jesus almost certainly wasn't born on December 25 or even in December. We simply don't know the exact date. But lack of certainty about Jesus' date of birth is certainly no reason to condemn

Christmas. We chose a date to commemorate the day our Lord and Savior entered the world, acknowledging the fact that he was born to die for the sins of the world.

I still think it's wrong to celebrate Christmas. Do you really think Christians should embrace this pagan holiday? I think we should be led by the Bible's specific teachings about holidays. And while we're on the subject, this will also apply to Easter.

So let's have a mini Bible study lesson, shall we?

To prepare, I highly recommend reading Colossians 2:1-15, as it leads into the verses we will focus on. It's a great passage about our freedom from legalism because of the person and work of Jesus Christ. Legalism is measuring your own or someone else's spirituality by the ability to keep *man-made* rules. Note the emphasis on man-made. We're NOT talking about things that the Bible clearly identifies as sin.

In Colossians 2:16-23, Paul gets specific.

> **Colossians 2:16-17**: So don't let anyone condemn you for what you

eat or drink, or for not celebrating certain holy days or new moon ceremonies or Sabbaths. For these rules are only shadows of the reality yet to come. And Christ himself is that reality.

Colossians 2:20-23: You have died with Christ, and he has set you free from the spiritual powers of this world. So why do you keep on following the rules of the world, such as, "Don't handle! Don't taste! Don't touch!"? Such rules are mere human teachings about things that deteriorate as we use them. These rules may seem wise because they require strong devotion, pious self-denial, and severe bodily discipline. But they provide no help in conquering a person's evil desires.

In summary, since you are free in Christ, don't allow anyone to judge you regarding the food you eat or the holidays you celebrate. This kind of legalism promotes a sense of self-righteousness, appearing to be spiritual while doing nothing to address the sin in our hearts.

Now **Romans 1:1-7** really hits the nail on the head.

> Accept other believers who are weak in faith, and don't argue with them about what they think is right or wrong. For instance, one person believes it's all right to eat anything. But another believer with a sensitive conscience will eat only vegetables.
>
> Those who feel free to eat anything must not look down on those who don't. And those who don't eat certain foods must not condemn those who do, for God has accepted them.
>
> Who are you to condemn someone else's servants? Their own master will judge whether they stand or fall. And with the Lord's help, they will stand and receive his approval.
>
> In the same way, **some think one day is more holy than another day, while others think every day is alike. You should each be fully convinced that whichever day you choose is acceptable.** *Those who*

worship the Lord on a special day do it to honor him.

Those who eat any kind of food do so to honor the Lord, since they give thanks to God before eating. And those who refuse to eat certain foods also want to please the Lord and give thanks to God. For we don't live for ourselves or die for ourselves.

This passage opens by admonishing Christians not to argue about doubtful issues, identifying those doubtful issues as food and holidays. So one person is a vegetarian; the other eats meat. One person eats pork; the other abstains. One person observes the Sabbath; the other does not. One person celebrates Christmas and Easter; the other considers them pagan and doesn't participate. Paul's conclusion on these issues? It's all good. *It. Does. Not. Matter.*

Let's summarize the lessons found in Romans 14:1-7

- If you choose not to celebrate a holiday, don't judge the person who chooses to indulge.

- If you feel free to celebrate a holiday, don't look down on those who restrict themselves.
- God accepts Christians even in their differences.
- God is your judge, not other people.
- Be ruled by your conscience and make up your own mind (Again, this applies to things that aren't clearly labeled as sin).

Notice Paul isn't telling people what to do (adhere to certain diets or not, observe certain holidays or not). His only concern is our attitude toward those who disagree with us. He forbids judging others by our own *preferences*. Christians must not compromise about anything clearly forbidden in Scripture, but they shouldn't create additional rules and make them equal to God's Word.

So, should you celebrate Christmas (or any other holiday)? Only if you want to! If your conscience bothers you, don't celebrate Christmas, but that doesn't mean you have to ruin everyone else's Christmas cheer.

Don't go around being a Scrinch (Scrooge/Grinch) ... or is Grooge better?

43. WHY DIDN'T JESUS DISCUSS HOMOSEXUALITY?

Here's an odd societal teaching: Jesus didn't preach against (or discuss) homosexuality; therefore, it must be ok. That's just nonsense. Jesus didn't intend to teach about every possible sin that could be committed. He spoke primarily about prevalent issues of the day and about issues that were frequently misunderstood by the Pharisees.

Remember that the Old Testament does address homosexuality (Leviticus 18:22 and 20:13), so in Jesus' mind, the issue is far from "unaddressed." The sin of homosexuality wasn't in doubt at the time among the Jews he was teaching, so Jesus didn't address it. However, the Apostle Paul traveled in circles where the issue did need to be addressed (Romans 1:24-27; 1 Corinthians 6:9-10). Also see Jude 1:7.

The argument that Jesus didn't teach against homosexuality is often made by people who don't otherwise follow Christ, but they are now suddenly concerned about what he had to say on this subject. They want to prove that if he didn't address it, it must be ok.

But this view sees the Bible as various parts that don't work together rather than as one comprehensive teaching. You see, it doesn't matter if Abraham said it, Moses said it, Isaiah said it, Jesus said it, or Paul said it. God said it all!

44. WHAT DOES IT MEAN TO BE BORN AGAIN?

In John 3:3-7, Jesus tells Nicodemus that no one can enter God's kingdom unless they are born again. The Greek word translated "again" can also be translated "above." So one who is born again or born from above is one born of God. Jesus goes on to explain that one must be born both of water and the Spirit. These terms could refer to both physical birth and spiritual birth, or both could be a metaphor referring to the Spirit.

Elsewhere, Jesus refers to living water (John 4:10-15; John 7:38), which is synonymous with the Spirit. We need to be born again because flesh gives birth to flesh, but only the Spirit can give birth to Spirit. And spiritual birth is required to enter the Kingdom of God.

45. WHAT DID JESUS TEACH ABOUT DIVORCE?

Jesus taught the following about divorce:

- God never intended divorce as an option, but he allowed it through Moses because of our stubbornness (Mark 10:1-9).
- Sexual immorality is legitimate grounds for divorce (Matthew 19:9). This certainly includes cheating. One could argue it includes things like pornography as well.
- Divorcing for other reasons causes both parties to commit adultery if they remarry (Mark 10:11-12).

So according to Jesus (and later Paul—see 1 Corinthians 7:10-16), there are legitimate grounds for divorce. However, divorce outside these parameters is a sin. As Christians, we should do everything we can to remain married, as that is God's will.

Now, many Christians are concerned about one or more divorces that have occurred in the past. But do not stress out about the past; simply repent and be forgiven. If you are married, don't deliberately get divorced. Do everything you can to stay married. Willfully divorcing is willfully sinning.

However, we're talking now about divorces that have already happened, and I've got a controversial word for you about that. Hear me, and hear me well. Contrary to what is taught in some churches, divorce is NOT an unforgivable sin.

The concern is more about Jesus' teaching that if you divorce someone for the wrong reason and you both get remarried, you have created the sin of adultery for you both. And this is true. But again, adultery is not an unforgivable sin either. We've seen that in action more than once in the Bible. David and Bathsheba and the woman caught in adultery come to mind.

Divorcing for the wrong reasons is a sin, and committing or causing someone to commit adultery is a sin. But just like any other sins, they can be forgiven.

So if you've gotten divorced and the fault was yours, repent and move on. You are forgiven. And if the divorce wasn't your fault, you are free and have no need of forgiveness. The other person left you and likely entered a new relationship at some point. This means they have committed adultery, leaving you free from being bound to them in marriage.

46. WHAT DID JESUS TEACH ABOUT PAYING TAXES?

Jesus taught that we are required to obey the laws of the land, so unfortunately, yes, we should pay our taxes. When he was asked this very question by the Pharisees, he responded by asking them to identify the image on their popular coin. When they identified the image as Caesar's, Jesus gave his famous quote: "Render to Caesar the things that are Caesar's and render to God the things that belong to God." Incidentally, Paul teaches this principle as well (Romans 13:6-7).

47. WHY DID THE PHARISEES HATE JESUS?

When Jesus began his public ministry, he upset the traditions and interpretation of laws upon which the Pharisees built their righteousness. But more than that, he exuded the kind of authority that put him on the same level as God (and, thus, over their own perceived authority). To the Pharisees, this was blasphemy because, in their eyes, he was only a man. They didn't believe that the reason he displayed God's authority was because he was, in fact, God himself.

48. DID JESUS TEACH AGAINST THE SABBATH?

No, Jesus didn't teach against the Sabbath — he kept the Sabbath himself. However, he did teach an expanded view of the Sabbath. The Sabbath is a hot-button issue among Christians, so I think it's important to study what the scripture says collectively about it rather than just focusing on our favorite verses to prove a point. What the Bible says about a subject can only be fully appreciated when we consider all the verses in unison. So let's start at the beginning.

The Sabbath in the Beginning

The first mention of the Sabbath was right after creation. When God rested on the seventh day (the Sabbath), he made the day holy. The next significant instance of the Sabbath is when it appears as the fourth law in the Ten Commandments. Because the Lord rested on the Sabbath and blessed it, the Israelites were to honor it as holy.

But there was another reason as well. Deuteronomy further explains that they were commanded to keep the Sabbath because God brought them out of slavery from Egypt. So we notice right away that this is the only commandment given with such a narrow focus: "You were slaves in Egypt, so keep the Sabbath."

Jesus' Teachings on the Sabbath

In the New Testament (Matthew 12:1-14, Luke 13:10-17, Luke 14:1-6, John 5:16-47), Jesus has several encounters with the Pharisees about the Sabbath. Now Jesus NEVER told anyone not to keep the Sabbath; however, he demonstrated by his actions that a shift was coming about, emphasizing that he was Lord over the Sabbath. In essence, he had implemented the Sabbath laws; therefore, he could set people straight regarding how to interpret them.

Not only that, he stated that the Sabbath was made for man, not man for the Sabbath. In other words, it's not meant to be a burden that we subject ourselves to; rather, it is subject to us.

The Disciples' Future Interpretation of the Sabbath

After Jesus was resurrected on the first day of the week (Sunday), the disciples started meeting on that day (Acts 20:6-7). This speaks volumes. They were good Jews and wouldn't take the Jewish laws lightly. But they switched their day of worship from Saturday to Sunday without even so much as a discussion on the matter.

Paul's Teaching on the Sabbath

Paul's behavior mirrors those of the disciples. He preached on a Sunday (1 Corinthians 16:1-4), though he still went to the synagogues to teach the Jews about Jesus. He didn't go there to teach Christians, because they had already started meeting on Sundays in each other's houses (Acts 17:2 and Acts 18:4).

As the Jews consistently rejected Paul's message, God ordained him as the Apostle to the Gentiles (non-Jews). When these Gentiles were being converted, the Jews wanted them to keep the Jewish law, but Paul had a lot to say on the subject, particularly regarding the Sabbath.

Romans 14:1-12 is a great passage to read regarding this subject, and we already touched on it in our discussion about holidays. Verses 5-6 say, "One person considers one day more sacred than another; another considers every day alike. Each of them should be fully convinced in their own mind. Whoever regards one day as special does so to the Lord...."

Paul further emphasizes this point in Colossians 2:8 & 2:13-23: Verses 16-17 state, "Therefore do not let anyone judge you by what you eat or drink, or with regard to a religious festival, a New Moon celebration or a Sabbath day...."

So as you can see, there is a progression in the Bible regarding the teaching of the Sabbath. After Jesus came, lots of things changed, and the Sabbath rule was one of them. The Sabbath isn't supposed to be burdensome (I must keep the Sabbath or else); instead, it's optional. Those who want to keep the Sabbath are free to do so, but they shouldn't judge others for not keeping it.

49. DID JESUS TEACH AGAINST THE LAW?

No, Jesus didn't teach against the law, but in that case, we're confronted with how to reconcile two of his statements: (1) Jesus didn't come to abolish the law and (2) Jesus came to fulfill the law (Matthew 5:17).

Consider this example: In your house, the law is that the dishes must be washed each night, and you have been given that responsibility. But one night you come home late from work and the dishes are already washed. Someone washed them on your behalf (*fulfilled* your responsibility to wash them).

Now this doesn't mean that the law of washing the dishes has been abolished.

That law still remains, but because it was fulfilled on your behalf, you don't have to wash them now.

But wait a minute! If Jesus kept the laws for us, doesn't that mean we don't have to keep any laws? Certainly not. You see, there are different types of laws. There are laws that we no longer have to keep because Jesus fulfilled our obligation once and for all. This applies to the sacrificial and ceremonial laws.

Now there's another type of law that I like to call the "**Now I'm Grown**" law. When I was a child, my mother wouldn't let me do certain things. I couldn't cook on a hot stove, go outside alone, or stay up late. In my teenage years, I could cook, go outside alone, and stay up late. However, even though I could go outside alone, I still had a curfew. And even though I could stay up late, I couldn't stay up all night.

But now I'm grown, and those laws simply don't apply to me anymore. It's not that the laws were bad, but they were only put in place for a particular purpose and for a particular time. They were put in place to guide me while I was immature. Those laws had an expiration date! They were temporary and never designed to be permanent. I was *always* meant to outgrow them.

In the same way, many of the laws God put in place were never meant to be permanent. God always intended that we would outgrow our need for them. When Jesus came, it was a big deal—his arrival was significant enough that some major things changed. It seems like we're sometimes afraid to admit that things changed from the Old Testament to the New Testament, but yes, things changed … for the better!

So how can we know what laws to follow now? A good rule of thumb is to give priority to the New Testament. The Bible is a progression of teachings, and teachings in the New Testament are more current than those in the Old Testament.

But if a law from the Old Testament is repeated in the New Testament, we must still abide by it. If an Old Testament law is not repeated, or if it's clearly stated that the law is no longer binding on us, then we're free from the obligation. (And yes, ALL the **moral** laws have carried over to the New Testament. Every one of them. Sorry! ☺).

50. WHAT OLD TESTAMENT PROPHECIES ABOUT CHRIST WERE FULFILLED?

Old Testament Prophecy	New Testament Fulfillment
"But you, Bethlehem Ephrathah, though you are small among the clans of Judah, out of you will come for me one who will be ruler over Israel, whose origins are from of old, from ancient times." **(Micah 5:2)**	So Joseph also went up from the town of Nazareth in Galilee to Judea, to Bethlehem the town of David, because he belonged to the house and line of David. He went there to register with Mary, who was pledged to be married to him and was expecting a child. While they were there, the time came for the baby to be born, and she gave birth to her firstborn, a son. She wrapped him in cloths and placed him in a manger, because there was no room for them in the inn. **(Luke 2:4–7)**
Therefore the Lord himself will give you a sign:	All this took place to fulfill what the Lord had said

Old Testament Prophecy	New Testament Fulfillment
The virgin will be with child and will give birth to a son, and will call him Immanuel. **(Isaiah 7:14)**	through the prophet: "The virgin will be with child and will give birth to a son, and they will call him Immanuel"—which means, "God with us." **(Matthew 1:22–23)**
Nevertheless, there will be no more gloom for those who were in distress. In the past he humbled the land of Zebulun and the land of Naphtali, but in the future he will honor Galilee of the Gentiles, by the way of the sea, along the Jordan. **(Isaiah 9:1)**	When Jesus heard that John had been put in prison, he returned to Galilee. Leaving Nazareth, he went and lived in Capernaum, which was by the lake in the area of Zebulun and Naphtali—to fulfill what was said through the prophet Isaiah. **(Matthew 4:12–14)**
I told them, "If you think it best, give me my pay; but if not, keep it." So they paid me thirty pieces of silver. **(Zechariah 11:12)**	Then one of the 12—the one called Judas Iscariot—went to the chief priests and asked, "What are you willing to give me if I hand him over to you?"

Old Testament Prophecy	New Testament Fulfillment
Even my close friend, whom I trusted, he who shared my bread, has lifted up his heel against me. **(Psalm 41:9)**	So they counted out for him thirty silver coins. From then on Judas watched for an opportunity to hand him over. **(Matthew 26:14–16)** While he was still speaking, Judas, one of the 12, arrived. With him was a large crowd armed with swords and clubs, sent from the chief priests and the elders of the people. Now the betrayer had arranged a signal with them: "The one I kiss is the man; arrest him." Going at once to Jesus, Judas said, "Greetings, Rabbi!" and kissed him. Jesus replied, "Friend, do what you came for." **(Matthew 26:47–50)**

Old Testament Prophecy	New Testament Fulfillment
Rejoice greatly, O Daughter of Zion! Shout, Daughter of Jerusalem! See, your king comes to you, righteous and having salvation, gentle and riding on a donkey, on a colt, the foal of a donkey. **(Zec 9:9)**	As they approached Jerusalem and came to Bethphage on the Mount of Olives, Jesus sent two disciples, saying to them, "Go to the village ahead of you, and at once you will find a donkey tied there, with her colt by her. Untie them and bring them to me. If anyone says anything to you, tell him that the Lord needs them, and he will send them right away." **(Matthew 21:1–3)**
But I am a worm and not a man, scorned by men and despised by the people. All who see me mock me; they hurl insults, shaking their heads:	The people stood watching, and the rulers even sneered at him. They said, "He saved others; let him save himself if he is the Christ of God, the Chosen One."

Old Testament Prophecy	New Testament Fulfillment
"He trusts in the LORD; let the LORD rescue him. Let him deliver him, since he delights in him." **(Psalm 22:6–8)**	The soldiers also came up and mocked him. They offered him wine vinegar and said, "If you are the king of the Jews, save yourself." There was a written notice above him, which read: THIS IS THE KING OF THE JEWS. One of the criminals who hung there hurled insults at him: "Aren't you the Christ? Save yourself and us!" **(Luke 23:35–39)**
They divide my garments among them and cast lots for my clothing. **(Psalm 22:18)**	When the soldiers crucified Jesus, they took his clothes, dividing them into four shares, one for each of them, with the undergarment remaining.

Old Testament Prophecy	New Testament Fulfillment
	This garment was seamless, woven in one piece from top to bottom. "Let's not tear it," they said to one another. "Let's decide by lot who will get it." This happened that the scripture might be fulfilled which said, "They divided my garments among them and cast lots for my clothing." So this is what the soldiers did. **(John 19:23–24)**
Therefore I will give him a portion among the great, and he will divide the spoils with the strong, because he poured out his life unto death, and was numbered with the transgressors.	One of the criminals who hung there hurled insults at him: "Aren't you the Christ? Save yourself and us!" But the other criminal rebuked him. "Don't you fear God," he said, "since you are under the same

Old Testament Prophecy	New Testament Fulfillment
For he bore the sin of many, and made intercession for the transgressors. **(Isaiah 53:12)**	sentence? We are punished justly, for we are getting what our deeds deserve. But this man has done nothing wrong." **(Luke 23:39–41)**
My strength is dried up like a potsherd, and my tongue sticks to the roof of my mouth; you lay me in the dust of death. **(Psalm 22:15)**	Later, knowing that all was now completed, and so that the Scripture would be fulfilled, Jesus said, "I am thirsty." A jar of wine vinegar was there, so they soaked a sponge in it, put the sponge on a stalk of the hyssop plant, and lifted it to Jesus' lips. **(John 19:28–29)**
And the LORD said to me, "Throw it to the potter"—the handsome price at which they priced me! So I took the thirty pieces of silver and threw them	When Judas, who had betrayed him, saw that Jesus was condemned, he was seized with remorse and returned the thirty silver coins to the chief priests

Old Testament Prophecy	New Testament Fulfillment
into the house of the LORD to the potter. **(Zechariah 11:13)**	and the elders. "I have sinned," he said, "for I have betrayed innocent blood." "What is that to us?" they replied. "That's your responsibility." So Judas threw the money into the temple and left. Then he went away and hanged himself. The chief priests picked up the coins and said, "It is against the law to put this into the treasury, since it is blood money." So they decided to use the money to buy the potter's field as a burial place for foreigners. **(Matthew 27:3–7)**
He was assigned a grave with the wicked, and with the rich in his death,	Later, Joseph of Arimathea asked Pilate for the body of Jesus… He was

Old Testament Prophecy	New Testament Fulfillment
though he had done no violence, nor was any deceit in his mouth. **(Isaiah 53:9)**	accompanied by Nicodemus... Taking Jesus' body, the two of them wrapped it, with the spices, in strips of linen. This was in accordance with Jewish burial customs. At the place where Jesus was crucified, there was a garden, and in the garden a new tomb, in which no one had ever been laid. **(John 19:38–41)**

51. DID JESUS EVER SIN?

Nope, not even a little bit, not even almost. Jesus never sinned, but he was tempted in every way that we are tempted (Hebrews 4:15). Contrary to popular belief, a temptation is not a sin. You can turn away from it and refuse to act on it and, thus, keep from sinning.

Yet even though Jesus committed no sin, he took our sin upon himself to save us (2 Corinthians 5:21; 1 John 3:5; 1 Peter 2:22). Without a *sinless* nature, he would have been disqualified as our Savior.

52. WHY DID JESUS HAVE TO BE TEMPTED?

Matthew 4:1-11, Mark 1:12-13, and Luke 4:1-13 tell the story of Jesus' temptation in the desert, but the Gospels don't explain why it was necessary. However, Paul tells us that Jesus was tempted so that he would experience humanity in every way. Experiencing temptation enables Jesus to empathize with our sufferings and help us through them (Hebrews 2:18; 4:15).

Not only that, but I think even Jesus had to be given a choice: To obey God or not, just like Adam and Eve. While the first Adam sinned and messed it up for all of us, the second Adam got it right and saved us.

53. WHY DID JESUS HAVE TO DIE?

Jesus had to die because all sin requires bloodshed from a pure vessel. Why? It's simply the way God set things up. The Old

Testament establishes this fact in great detail. It's a little odd, maybe, especially for us in this day and age. However, I'm sure God had his reasons, and one day we can ask him about it.

In the Old Testament, God set up a system whereby a flawless animal would shed its blood to atone for the sins of the people. But this system was never meant to be permanent. The repetitious nature made it less than ideal. On a daily, weekly, and yearly basis, people had to constantly make atonement for their sins by shedding the blood of an animal.

But God always planned to provide a once-and-for-all sacrifice, and that sacrifice was his son, Jesus Christ. The bloodshed of one who was flawless was still required, and Jesus satisfied that requirement; therefore, his blood was able to cleanse our sin once and for all. This is why the sacrificial system begins to disappear after Jesus' death on the cross.

54. WHY IS JESUS CALLED THE SON OF DAVID?

There are two primary reasons Jesus was called the Son of David:

- **He is David's physical descendant:** Matthew 1:1; Matthew 1:2-20; Luke 1:27,32. Jesus' bloodline was very important because God had established way back in the Old Testament that David's reign would be everlasting, through his descendants. So anyone who took the position of king had to meet the qualifications. They had to be of the line of David.

- **He is the promised Messiah of David's line**: Isaiah 16:5; Psalm 89:1-4; Isaiah 9:7. It was prophesied that from the tribe of Judah, the tribe of David, One would come to bring the new kingdom to Israel.

In an interesting conversation with the Pharisees, Jesus pointed out the irony that the Messiah is both the Son of David and the Lord of David (See Luke 20:41-44).

55. WHY IS JESUS CALLED OUR HIGH PRIEST?

Jesus is called our High Priest in Hebrews 2:17 and 4:14. The best way to understand this is to first evaluate the role of the High Priest. When God gave the Law at Mount Sinai, he set apart the tribe of Levi as his priests. From the priests, he chose Aaron (and his descendants) to serve as High Priest.

Once a year, the High Priest entered the Most Holy Place on the Day of Atonement to make sacrifices for himself and for the people. In this way, their sins were cleansed. The High Priest stood as a representative between God and the people. In the same way, Jesus made atonement for our sins on the cross, standing before God and shielding us from the consequences of our sins.

After Jesus' death, the veil of the temple was torn in two pieces, indicating that a High Priest was no longer necessary to go behind the veil and make atonement for the people. Jesus now served that role as the "mediator between God and mankind" (1 Timothy 2:5).

56. WHY DID JOHN CALL JESUS THE LAMB OF GOD?

John the Baptist calls Jesus the Lamb of God in John 1:29. This was a reference to the lamb that was slaughtered at Passover. We find in the book of Exodus that on the night the Israelites left Egypt, God instructed them to slaughter a lamb without defect and place some of its blood on the door frames. When God saw the blood on each house, he would "pass over" that house and spare the lives of its inhabitants. The Israelites observed this ritual once a year at the appointed time.

Just as the blood of the Passover spared the lives of the Israelites on that fateful night, the blood of Jesus spared our lives as well. Just as the blood of the Passover lamb allowed the angel of death to pass over the Israelites' homes, the blood of Jesus allows God's judgment to pass over our sins.

57. WHY ARE BELIEVERS CALLED CHRISTIANS?

The word Christian has its origins in the Bible and is therefore a biblical term.

Acts chapter 11 describes the ministry of Barnabas and Saul in Antioch. They taught there for a year, and many people were added to the church. It was at Antioch that the term "Christian" was first used to refer to followers of Christ. Christian comes from the Latin word *Christianos*, which means one who identifies with Christ and his teachings. The term is used two other times in the New Testament:

- **Acts 26:28**—Herod Agrippa asks whether Paul really thinks he will persuade him to become a Christian.
- **1 Peter 4:16**—Peter encourages those who suffer for being a Christian.

58. IF JESUS WAS A JEW, WHY AREN'T CHRISTIANS JEWISH?

At Mount Sinai, God made a covenant with the people of Israel. However, this covenant was only a precursor of a new covenant that God planned to give his people. Jeremiah 31:31-34 prophesied a time when the Lord would make a new covenant with the house of Israel, a law he would write in their minds and on their hearts.

The old covenant was fulfilled when Jesus Christ completed his mission on earth, so the new covenant (known as the New Testament) represents God's new covenant with his people. Hebrews 8:13 quotes the Jeremiah passage above and further explains that "by calling this covenant "'new,'" he has made the first one obsolete; and what is obsolete and outdated will soon disappear.

So the Bible itself naturally divides believers into Jewish (Old Testament) and Christian (New Testament). Many of the Jews rejected Jesus and his message, so Paul brought his message to the Gentiles (that's most of us), and they became known as Christians.

CHAPTER FIVE

JESUS' DIVINITY

59. WHAT DOES PHILIPPIANS 2:5-11 MEAN WHEN IT STATES THAT JESUS EMPTIED HIMSELF?

Depending on which translation you read, Philippians 2:5-11 states that Jesus "emptied himself" or "made himself nothing." I prefer "emptied himself," as I think it paints a more vivid picture of what actually took place. But what does it mean? It means that although Jesus had all the attributes and power of God, he didn't use that authority to his advantage. Instead, he freely gave up the equality with God that he was entitled to. He gave up his position of power and became a servant instead. So Jesus didn't get rid of his divine attributes but simply chose to subdue them and act only according to God's instructions while he was on earth.

60. WHAT IS THE RELATIONSHIP BETWEEN JESUS AND THE ARCHANGEL MICHAEL?

A popular religious denomination circulates the teaching that Jesus is really the Archangel Michael. However, nothing could be further from the truth. This teaching doesn't exist anywhere in Scripture. Jesus is the Son of God and divine in nature, but who is Michael?

The angel Michael is one of several archangels and is probably their leader. He is mentioned in Daniel 10:13, 21; Daniel 12:1; Jude 9; and Revelation 12:7-9 and is credited with leading the army that cast Satan and his angels from heaven. So Michael is an angel, a created being, while Jesus is divine and eternal—definitely not a created being.

61. IF JESUS WAS BORN OF A HUMAN, HOW DID HE ESCAPE HUMANITY'S SINFUL NATURE?

Original sin refers to the fact that Adam and Eve sinned. This left a stain deep in the fabric of their humanity. Therefore, everyone born after them inherited a sin nature. I believe the answer is found in the fact that

Mary did not conceive Jesus—the Holy Spirit did (Matthew 1:20). Mary only served as a surrogate. As John 3:6 states, Spirit gives birth to Spirit; it can't give birth to flesh.

62. DID JESUS DIE FOR EVERYONE?

Yes, Jesus died for everyone. John 3:16 says that God so loved the world that he gave his one and only son. The *world* means everybody, although not everybody will accept the gift that God has given. A gift can be refused, right? So Jesus offers salvation to everyone, but not everyone wants it because of the price that comes with it—serving Jesus as Lord.

63. WHAT DOES IT MEAN THAT JESUS WAS A LITTLE LOWER THAN THE ANGELS (PSALM 8:5; HEBREWS 2:7)?

When Jesus entered the earth, he left the heavenly realm and the majesty that he had there to become a human (Philippians 2:7). Although he was rich, he became poor (1 Corinthians 8:9). Although he gave us the Law, he became subject to that Law (Galatians 4:4). Humans are lower in stature than angels, so it simply means that Jesus, who is really above the angels, became lower than them to bring us salvation.

64. HOW CAN JESUS AND THE BIBLE BOTH BE THE WORD OF GOD?

Jesus is called the Word of God (John 1:1) as a *physical* expression of God's message. In the same way, the Bible is called God's Word as a *written* expression of his message.

65. WHY IS JESUS' RESURRECTION FROM THE DEAD SIGNIFICANT?

Many things Jesus did serve as examples for or identification with believers: He was baptized to demonstrate what he wanted us to do, he was tempted to experience our suffering, and ultimately, he was raised from the dead. By being raised from the dead, Jesus gave us the assurance that we too would be raised from the dead. Not only does it give the believer assurance of resurrection, it provides proof that Jesus is the Son of God.

66. WHAT IS THE SIGNIFICANCE OF JESUS REFERRING TO HIMSELF AS "I AM"?

In John 8:56-59, Jesus called himself *I Am* when comparing himself to Abraham. The Pharisees looked up to Abraham, but Jesus pointed out that he existed before Abraham and was therefore superior. The *I Am* statement also demonstrated to the Pharisees that Jesus equated himself with the Great I Am of the Old Testament (Exodus 3:14). That's why their reaction was to stone him.

67. WHAT DOES IT MEAN IN JOHN 3:16 THAT JESUS IS GOD'S ONLY BEGOTTEN SON?

"Only begotten is a term used in the King James Version of the Bible. Most current translations merely say "only son" or "one and only son." The meaning is that God had only one Son, and he gave him to the world to offer eternal life.

68. WHAT ARE SOME OTHER NAMES AND TITLES FOR JESUS CHRIST?

Much like God, Jesus Christ has multiple names in the Bible, both in the Old and New

Testament. Here are others that weren't already mentioned:

Light of the World: (John 8:12)

Prince of Peace: (Isaiah 9:6)

Alpha and Omega: (Revelation 1:8; 22:13)

Bread of Life: (John 6:35; 6:48)

Good Shepherd: (John 10:11,14)

King of kings and Lord of lords (Revelation 17:14, 19:16)

Bright Morning Star (Revelation 22:16)

Mighty God (Isaiah 9:6)

69. WHY IS JESUS CALLED THE SECOND ADAM?

There are two types of bodies: natural and spiritual. God made the first man, Adam, from dust and gave him the breath of life. But Jesus is not from the dust; he came from heaven. He always existed and was himself the giver of life. In the same way that Adam was the first human, Jesus was the first of those who will be raised from the dead and given a new body and eternal life (1 Corinthians 15:45-49).

Where the first Adam messed up and introduced sin into the world, the second Adam, Jesus, came to save the world from its sin.

70. WHAT DOES COLOSSIANS 1:15-21 MEAN WHEN IT SAYS THAT JESUS IS THE "FIRSTBORN" OVER CREATION?

When we read that Jesus is the "firstborn," our initial thought might be his physical birth. However, that's not what the term refers to. It refers instead to Jesus' relationship to God. It means that he existed before the creation of all things and is therefore superior to them.

71. IS THE TERM "TRINITY" IN THE BIBLE?

The word trinity never appears in the Bible; nevertheless, the concept is prevalent throughout. The trinity is the idea that there is only one God, but he exists in three persons or three modes of operation. He is *one* as to his essence but there is plurality as to his operation. Here are some scriptures that support the idea of the Trinity:

A. Each Member of the Trinity Is Identified as an Agent in Creation.

- In Genesis, **God** speaks his creation into existence and the **Spirit** hovers over the waters (Genesis 1:1-2). Later, God speaks in the plural: *"Let us make man"* (Genesis 1:26). This is similar to **Jesus'** statement in John 14:23—note the plural pronouns: *Jesus replied, "Anyone who loves me will obey my teaching. My Father will love them, and **we** will come to them and make **our** home with them."*
- Hebrews 11:3 states that the universe was formed at **God's** command, but Colossians 1:16-17 and John 1:3 say all things were created through **Jesus Christ**.

B. The Members of the Trinity Are Often Used Interchangeably or in Unison.

- Matthew 28:19 admonishes us to baptize in the name of the **Father**, **Son**, and **Holy Spirit**.
- In John 15:26, **Jesus** says he will send the **Spirit** from the **Father**.
- In John 16:7, **Jesus** says the **Spirit** can't come unless he goes. Why? Well, you don't need both. The Spirit

was only necessary once Jesus wasn't with the disciples any longer.
- In Acts 5:3-4, Peter first tells Ananias that he has lied to the **Holy Spirit**, but later he says he lied to **God**. Both were true!

72. WHAT DID JESUS MEAN WHEN HE IDENTIFIED HIMSELF AS THE RESURRECTION AND THE LIFE?

In calling himself the resurrection and the life, Jesus pointed to several truths:

- The Son has life within himself, and he can give that life to whoever he wishes.
- Those who die believing in Jesus (as Lazarus had done) will ultimately live.
- Those who live and believe in Jesus will never really die (spiritually).

73. IS JESUS THE ONLY WAY TO GOD?

Yes, Jesus is the only way to God. It's politically *incorrect*, but it's biblically *correct*. Consider the following:

John 3:18: Whoever believes in him is not condemned, but whoever does not believe stands condemned already because they have not believed in the name of God's one and only Son.

John 3:36: Whoever believes in the Son has eternal life, but whoever rejects the Son will not see life, for God's wrath remains on them.

John 6:45: "... Everyone who has heard the Father and learned from him comes to me."

John 8:19: "You do not know me or my Father," Jesus replied. "If you knew me, you would know my Father also."

John 8:42: Jesus said to them, "If God were your Father, you would love me…"

John 14:6: "I am the Way, the Truth, and the Life. No man comes to the Father except through me."

John 14:7: "If you really know me, you will know my Father as well…."

John 14:9: "….Anyone who has seen me has seen the Father…."

John 17:3: Now this is eternal life: that they know you, the only true God, and Jesus Christ, whom you have sent.

1 John 4:2–3: This is how you can recognize the Spirit of God: Every spirit that acknowledges that Jesus Christ has come in the flesh is from God, but every spirit that does not acknowledge Jesus is not from God. This is the spirit of the antichrist....

1 John 4:15: If anyone acknowledges that Jesus is the Son of God, God lives in them and they in God.

1 John 5:1: Everyone who believes that Jesus is the Christ is born of God....

1 John 5:9–12: We accept human testimony, but God's testimony is greater because it is the testimony of God, which he has given about his Son. Whoever believes in the Son of God accepts this testimony. Whoever does not believe God has made him out to be a liar, because they have not believed the testimony God has given about his Son. And this is the testimony: God has given us eternal life, and this life is in his Son. Whoever has the Son has life; whoever does not have the Son of God does not have life.

That's 13 scriptures that reinforce a single truth. There's only ONE way to God, through our Lord and Savior Jesus Christ. Don't let the politically correct views of the world fool you; the only way to get to God is *through* Jesus, not *around* him. No one can say "I believe in God, but I don't believe in Jesus Christ." The Bible teaches it's all or nothing. It's both of them or none of them.

We are instructed to enter through the narrow gate. For wide is the way that leads to destruction and many enter through it ... but narrow is the way that leads to life, and only a few find it (Matthew 7:13-14).

74. WHY IS JESUS CALLED CHRIST?

The word *Christ* comes from the Greek word *christos*, which means "anointed." It corresponds to the Hebrew word translated "Messiah." When Jesus is called "Christ," he is being called "the anointed one." *Christ* is not a name but a title. And this title is used for Jesus more often than any other in the New Testament.

The title Christ is so often paired with the name of Jesus that it has virtually become synonymous with his last name. One does not normally refer to Jesus as "Jesus bar Joseph," which would probably have been his legal name. Rather, his full name is considered "Jesus Christ." Because the term Christ is perceived to be a name, its full significance may be lost. But we must remember that he is literally Jesus, the Christ, the anointed one.

75. WHY IS JESUS CALLED LORD?

Christ is the most-often-used title for Jesus in the New Testament. The second-most-frequent designation for him is *Lord*. This title has a direct relationship to the Old Testament, as it was also used for God, where it called attention to God's absolute rule over the earth.

In Matthew 22:44, Jesus receives the title Lord and is elevated to the right hand of God and given all authority in heaven and earth. His disciples, countless others, and even Jesus himself consistently referred to him as Lord (Matthew 14:28; Mark 2:28; Luke 2:11). So Jesus is given a title that formerly had been reserved for God the Father. And that leads us into the next question.

76. IS JESUS GOD?

Yes, Jesus is God in the flesh. The God of the universe humbled himself and came down to earth in the form of a man. Many scriptures support this fact:

A. BOTH JESUS AND GOD ARE IDENTIFIED AS THE CREATOR.

- **John 1:1-3**: In the beginning was the Word, and the Word was with God, and the Word was God. He was with God in the beginning. *Through him all things were made; without him nothing was made that has been made.* (*The Word being spoken of here is Jesus*).

- **Colossians 1:16–17**: *For by him all things were created: things in heaven and on earth, visible and invisible,* whether thrones or powers or rulers or authorities; all things were created by him and for him. (*"Him" refers to Jesus*).

- **Hebrews 11:3**—By faith we understand *that the universe was formed at God's command,* so that what is seen was not made out of what was visible.

- **Hebrews 1:1-2**: In the past God spoke to our forefathers through the prophets at many times and in various ways, but in these last days he has spoken to us by *his Son, whom he appointed heir of all things, and through whom he made the universe.*

B. JESUS RESPONDS AS IF HE IS GOD

- **John 14:6-9** - Jesus answered, "I am the way and the truth and the life. No one comes to the Father except through me. If you really know me, you will know my Father as well. From now on, you do know him and have seen him."

- Philip said, "Lord, show us the Father and that will be enough for us."

Jesus answered: "Don't you know me, Philip, even after I have been among you such a long time? Anyone who has seen me has seen the Father. How can you say, 'Show us the Father'?

When Philip says, "Show us the Father," Jesus replies, "Don't you know me." Stop and think about the full significance of that for a moment. Then Jesus states that to see him is to see the Father—to know him is to know the Father. I don't think we can get much clearer than that!

C. BOTH GOD AND JESUS ARE IDENTIFIED AS *I AM*

- **Exodus 3:13-15** – Moses said to God, "Suppose I go to the Israelites and say to them, 'The God of your fathers has sent me to you,' and they ask me, 'What is his name?' Then what shall I tell them?" God said to Moses, "I AM WHO I AM. This is what you are to say to the Israelites: '**I AM** has sent me to you.'"

- **John 8:54-59** - Jesus replied, "If I glorify myself, my glory means nothing. My Father, whom you claim as your God, is the one who glorifies me. Though you do not know him, I know him. If I said I did not, I would be a liar like you, but I do know him and obey his word. Your father Abraham rejoiced at the thought of seeing my day; he saw it and was glad."

> "You are not yet fifty years old," they said to him, "and you have seen Abraham!"
>
> "Very truly I tell you," Jesus answered, "before Abraham was born, **I Am**!"
>
> At this, they picked up stones to stone him, but Jesus hid himself, slipping away from the temple grounds.

Why did the Jews want to stone Jesus? Because they understood that he was identifying himself with the Great I Am of Exodus.

D. JESUS FORGIVES SINS WITH THE AUTHORITY OF GOD HIMSELF

MATTHEW 9:2-8, MARK 2:1-12, LUKE 5:17-26 (Taken from *The Chronological Word Truth Life Bible: Behold the Lamb ~ A Harmony of the Gospels*)

> A few days later, Jesus went to Capernaum again, and the people heard that he had returned home. So many people had gathered that there was no room left, not even outside the door, and he preached the Word to them.

The Pharisees and teachers of the law were also sitting there, having come from all the villages of Galilee, Judea, and Jerusalem.

Now the power of the Lord was present for him to heal the sick. Four men arrived carrying a paralytic. They tried to take him into the house to lay him before Jesus, but they couldn't because of the crowd. So they dug through the tiles on the roof and made a hole right above Jesus. Then they lowered the paralyzed man on his mat into the middle of the crowd, right in front of Jesus.

Jesus was impressed with their faith and said to the paralytic, "Son, be encouraged; your sins are forgiven."

The Pharisees and the teachers of the law thought to themselves, *Who is this man who speaks blasphemy? No one can forgive sins but God alone.*

Jesus knew immediately what they were thinking. "Why do you entertain evil thoughts?" he asked. "Is it easier to say 'Your sins are forgiven' or to say 'Get up and walk'? But now you will know that the Son of Man has authority on earth to forgive sins."

So he said to the paralytic, "Get up, take your mat, and go home."

Immediately the man got up in front of everyone and went home praising God.

They were amazed and praised God for giving such authority. "We've never seen anything like this!" they said.

The focus of this passage is the bold section. I can forgive you for hurting me or taking something that belongs to me. But if you sin against someone unrelated to me, it's very presumptuous for me to say "I forgive you." The Jews recognized this, and that's why they said only God can forgive sins. But Jesus revealed that he did have God's authority to forgive sins, and he demonstrated this *invisible* authority by the *physical* evidence of healing the paralytic.

E. JESUS IS GOD IN HIS VERY NATURE

Philippians 2:5-11: In your relationships with one another, have the same mindset as **Christ Jesus: Who, being in very nature God**, did not consider equality with God something to be used to his own advantage; rather, he made himself nothing by taking the very nature of a servant, being made in human likeness. And being found in appearance as a man, he humbled himself by becoming obedient to death—even death on a cross!

Therefore God exalted him to the highest place and gave him the name that is above every name, that at the name of Jesus every knee should bow, in heaven and on earth and under the earth, and every tongue acknowledge that Jesus Christ is Lord, to the glory of God the Father.

77. WHY IS JESUS CALLED "THE WORD" IN JOHN 1:1?

The term translated *Word* is the common Greek word *logos*, which meant "speaking, message, or words." John chose the term because it was familiar to his readers, but he also infused it with his own meaning.

The term was well known by those of both Greek and Jewish backgrounds. For the Greeks, who held to a theistic (God-focused) view of the universe, the *Word* was how God revealed himself to the world. For those with a pantheist (universe-focused) view, the *Word* was the principle that held the world together and provided men with wisdom.

In the Greek translation of the Old Testament, the *Word* could be used both for the means by which God had created the world (Psalm 33:6) and the way through which he had revealed himself to the world (Jeremiah 1:4; Ezekiel 1:3; Amos 3:1).

By the time of John's writing, the *Word* is close to being recognized as a personal being. And John claimed that this *Word* was indeed the God of creation, the ultimate mind of the universe who had taken on human form. Gary Vanderet states, "John intends that the entire book be read in light of this verse. The deeds and the words of Jesus are the deeds and words of God."

78. IF JESUS IS GOD, WHY IS HE CALLED THE SON OF GOD?

Son of God is one of the titles frequently applied to Jesus in the Gospels. Because Christians claim Jesus is God, the title "Son of God" can be particularly confusing. The simple answer may not be completely satisfying, but here's the basic truth: Jesus is both God and the Son of God. But let's dig into the subject further.

Jesus is the Son of God because of:

- **His divine origin and divinity**—Luke 1:32-35; John 5:18; John 17:5, 24
- **His intimate relationship with the Father**—Matthew 3:17; John 1:18; Mark 14:36—Note that "Abba" was a term of intimacy that children used with their own fathers.
- **His knowledge of the Father's will**—Matthew 11:25-27; John 15:15
- **His obedience to the Father's mission**—Matthew 26:42; Matthew 3:13-17; Matthew 4:1-11
- **His sharing in the Father's work**—John 3:34; John 5:17,21-26; John 12:49-50; John 14:11

- His role as promised Messiah—Ps 89:26-27; Isa 9:6-7; Luke 4:41
- His sharing the Father's character and essence—Heb 1:3 John 5:26; John 10:30; John 17:5

So the term Son of God in the New Testament communicates God's endorsement, commission, and empowerment of Jesus. It emphasizes Jesus' personal intimacy with the Father and obedience to the will of the Father. It speaks of the unique relationship Jesus has with his Father and of his mission to enable his people to become God's children through faith in him.

Jesus is both the Son of God and God with us (Immanuel) (Matthew 1:23). He is "God the only Son, who is at the Father's side" (John 1:18).

Perhaps Hebrews. 1:3 best communicates the idea of Jesus being both Son of God and God at the same time: *The Son is the radiance of God's glory and the exact representation of his being, sustaining all things by his powerful word. After he had provided purification for sins, he sat down at the right hand of the Majesty in heaven.*

Like God, Jesus has many different titles, but no matter which title you call him, he is *"in very nature God"* (Philippians 2:6).

79. IF JESUS IS GOD, WHY IS HE CALLED THE SON OF MAN?

The *Son of Man* title is interesting because it is the third-most-frequently-used title for Jesus in the New Testament, and it's Jesus' favorite title to refer to himself. We've already demonstrated that Jesus is both God and God's Son. Now we'll see how he can also be the Son of Man, and what that really means.

The title *Son of Man* is often assumed to refer to the humble humanity of Jesus, but it is much more than that. References to the Son of Man can be found in the books of Revelation (1:12-16; 5:11-12) and Daniel.

In the book of Daniel, the Son of Man appears before the Ancient of Days and is given authority, glory, and sovereign power; all nations and peoples of every language worshiped him. His dominion is an everlasting dominion that will not pass away, and his kingdom is one that will never be destroyed (Daniel 7:14).

Here, the Son of Man is a heavenly being who will exercise the role of supreme judge. He was a messianic figure of splendor and power. So whenever Jesus references the Son of Man, he is calling attention to this image.

80. IF JESUS IS GOD, WHO DID HE PRAY TO?

Jesus, as the Son, prayed to God as the Father. Even before Jesus became human, the two existed in an eternal relationship, separate but the same in nature. So it was totally possible to have God both in heaven and on earth, able to communicate one to another.

81. IF JESUS IS GOD, WHY DIDN'T HE KNOW THE DATE OF HIS RETURN?

In Matthew 24:35-37, Jesus said that no one except the Father knows the time of his return, not even Jesus himself. The explanation is that even though Jesus was God, he often voluntarily confined himself to the limits of humanity. For whatever reason, knowledge of his return is one of those privileges Jesus chose not to avail himself of while he was in human form. But after he was resurrected, he retained his rightful place of glory and was once again all-knowing.

82. IF JESUS IS GOD, WHY DID HE SAY THE FATHER WAS GREATER THAN HE?

Jesus made the striking statement in John 14:28 that the Father is greater than he. But if both are God, how can one be greater than the other? Again, this statement points to Jesus' emptying of himself. He had all the rights of the Father and was equal to him, yet in his humanity on earth, he didn't take full advantage of those rights. Instead he opted to be humble and to be led by his Father.

The Father was greater positionally (1) because he was in heaven, in the place of glory and (2) because he was fully divine while Jesus was part human. As a man, Jesus subjected himself to God just as we do, but this didn't make him any less divine.

83. IF JESUS IS GOD, HOW COULD GOD FORSAKE HIM ON THE CROSS?

In Matthew 27:46, Jesus says, "My God, my God, why have you forsaken me." This is actually a quote from the first part of Psalm 22:1, but the words do indicate that Jesus had a real sense of separation from the Father before he died.

2 Corinthians 5:21 says that Jesus had no sin, yet God made him become sin. What does that mean? It means God laid the blame for our sin on Christ. Jesus stood in the place of sinners and endured our punishment. So it's no surprise that Jesus would feel separated from God because of the weight of sin that he carried. Just as sin separates us from God, it temporarily separated Jesus from God, not in a real, physical way, but certainly emotionally.

84. IF JESUS IS GOD, HOW COULD HE BE TEMPTED?

James 1:13 says that God can't be tempted by evil and that he himself doesn't tempt anyone. So how do we reconcile this with Jesus being tempted in the wilderness? The key is to understand that the word translated "tempted" doesn't mean the same thing every time it's used.

One sense of the word *tempt* is *put to the test*. We see this when the Israelites constantly tempted (tested) God when they wandered in the desert. When Satan tempted Jesus in the desert, he was testing Jesus' faith and obedience to see whether he would disobey God.

Another sense of the word is *enticed to do wrong*, and it is in this way that God can never be tempted. He will never consider giving in to sin, nor will he ever cause us to give in to sin.

85. WHO RAISED JESUS FROM THE DEAD?

God raised Jesus from the dead; however, Jesus also raised himself from the dead. Though the statements may seem contradictory, both are true. By now, it should make a little more sense because we've already established that Jesus is God.

In John 10:17-18, Jesus states that he has the authority to lay down his life and he has the authority to take it up again. In John 2:19, he tells the Jewish leaders that if they destroyed his temple, he would raise it again in three days. However, other scriptures state that God raised Jesus from the dead (Acts 2:24; Acts 3:15; Colossians 2:12). Jesus is God, which is why they can be referred to in this way interchangeably.

CHAPTER SIX

FINAL DAYS

86. WHAT WAS THE SEQUENCE OF EVENTS DURING THE LAST WEEK OF JESUS' DEATH?

Jesus' final week begins on a **Saturday**, when Mary of Bethany anoints him at Simon the Leper's house. The next day, **Sunday**, he rides into Jerusalem on a donkey and is welcomed by the crowds shouting "Hosanna." On **Monday** and **Tuesday**, Jesus clears the Temple and has multiple encounters with the Jewish leaders. On **Wednesday**, things heat up. Jesus tells his disciples that he will soon be crucified, and the Jewish leaders begin their plot to arrest him. During this time, Judas offers to hand Jesus over to them.

On **Thursday** evening, Jesus observes the Passover/Last Supper with his disciples in the upper room. He has his last words with them as they leave the room and enter the Garden of Gethsemane. Later, Judas arrives, leading a group of soldiers, and he betrays Jesus with a kiss. The soldiers arrest Jesus and lead him to Annas, the father-in-law of High Priest Caiaphas. Annas questions Jesus. While Jesus is being questioned, Peter denies him three times.

Early **Friday** morning, Annas sends Jesus to Caiaphas and the council of Jewish leaders. They question Jesus and decide he should be sentenced to death; meanwhile, Judas hangs himself. While it is still early morning, the Jewish leaders decide to take Jesus to Pilate, who ultimately sentences Jesus to death.

Jesus is crucified around 9am. After that, there is a flurry of activity as soldiers divide Jesus' clothing, Jesus saves the repentant criminal, the crowds insult him, and he entrusts his mother to the apostle John.

Around noon that **Friday**, all goes quiet and darkness covers the land for three hours. At 3pm Jesus gives a final shout of victory from the cross and gives up his Spirit. Joseph of Arimathea and Nicodemus claim his body and bury it in Joseph's tomb located nearby.

It is now Friday evening, and the Sabbath is about to begin. The women who witnessed the crucifixion and observed the burial go home and prepare spices, and then they rest on the Sabbath.

On **Saturday**, Pilate grants the request to guard Jesus' tomb. Finally, the women go to the tomb early on **Sunday** morning and find it empty, and two angels tell them Jesus has risen from the dead!

Mary Magdalene stays behind and encounters Jesus. She then goes to tell the disciples he is alive, but they don't believe her. So Peter and John run to the tomb. Later, Jesus appears to all of the disciples and they finally believe he is alive.

87. WHY DID THE JEWISH LEADERS WANT TO KILL JESUS?

Jesus' ministry consisted of many debates and discussions with the Jewish leaders. They accused him of breaking the law, particularly the Sabbath; they accused him of being demon-possessed; and they accused him of making himself equal with God. At the heart of the issue, they were simply jealous.

Jesus arrived on the scene exuding the kind of authority that only God had, and he upset their sense of their own authority. Jesus' miracles did nothing to change their hearts; instead, they feared Jesus and his power. That's why the raising of Lazarus was the last straw. So many people believed in him after witnessing such a spectacular miracle, and the Jewish leaders were determined to kill him because of it.

88. WHY DID THE JEWS GO TO PILATE INSTEAD OF KILLING JESUS THEMSELVES?

The Jewish leaders weren't satisfied with merely punishing Jesus. They wanted him dead. However, since they were under Roman rule, they had to follow Roman laws. Only the government could carry out the death penalty (John 18:31-32), so the Jews had to think of a reason for the Romans to crucify Jesus.

89. WHY DID JUDAS ISCARIOT BETRAY JESUS?

I believe we would all like the answer to the question of why Judas Iscariot betrayed Jesus. How could someone who associated so closely with Jesus ultimately betray him? The only thing we can do is take our clues from the Gospels.

It seems Judas was greedy, and his heart was hard. He objected to the woman who had poured expensive perfume on Jesus' feet, and he also stole from the money box (John 12:1-6). Finally, Judas sold Jesus for 30 pieces of silver. Clearly, being around Jesus did nothing to soften his heart and change him.

It's probably fair to say that Judas didn't expect the Jewish leaders to put Jesus to death. They didn't let Judas in on their full plans, and they made the final decision to kill Jesus after Judas had turned Jesus over to them.

When Judas saw that Jesus was condemned to death, he clearly understood that he had gone too far, which is why he tried to give back the money. But it was too late to undo what he had begun. He couldn't face himself and he committed suicide. Judas left a sad legacy. He is never mentioned in the Gospels without being identified as Jesus' betrayer.

90. DID JUDAS GO TO HELL FOR BETRAYING JESUS?

Yes, I believe Judas did (or will) go to hell for betraying Jesus. Jesus said that Judas was destined for destruction (John 17:12) and that it would have been better if he hadn't been born (Matthew 26:24). His apparent remorse was only guilt and not true repentance. As Paul said in 2 Corinthians 7:10, "Godly sorrow brings repentance that leads to salvation and leaves no regret, but worldly sorrow brings death."

We see this principle in action when we compare Judas and Peter. Judas betrayed Jesus, and Peter denied Jesus. Both were sorry. But Judas was condemned and Peter was restored (John 21:15-19). From the outside, both apostles messed up and both seemed sorry. Judas tried to give back the money and then hung himself. Peter wept bitterly (Matthew 26:75). Indeed, Judas' sorrow seems more significant when you compare their actions. But only God knows the true heart of man, and obviously, their hearts were very different.

91. WHO WAS RESPONSIBLE FOR JESUS' DEATH?

Well, here's a better question: Is there anyone who *wasn't* responsible? According to the Bible, the following people had a role to play in Jesus' death.

THE JEWISH LEADERS

> **Matthew 26:3-4**: Then the chief priests and the elders of the people assembled in the palace of the high priest, whose name was Caiaphas, and they schemed to arrest Jesus secretly and kill him.

THE ROMANS

> **Matthew 27:27-31**: Then the governor's soldiers took Jesus into the Praetorium and gathered the whole company of soldiers around him. They stripped him and put a scarlet robe on him, and then twisted together a crown of thorns and set it on his head. They put a staff in his right hand. Then they knelt in front of

him and mocked him. "Hail, king of the Jews!" they said. They spit on him, and took the staff and struck him on the head again and again. After they had mocked him, they took off the robe and put his own clothes on him. Then they led him away to crucify him.

JUDAS

Luke 22:48: But Jesus asked him, "Judas, are you betraying the Son of Man with a kiss?"

Luke 22:22: The Son of Man will go as it has been decreed. But woe to that man who betrays him!

THE PEOPLE OF ISRAEL

Matthew 27:22-25: "What shall I do, then, with Jesus who is called the Messiah?" Pilate asked.

They all answered, "Crucify him!"

"Why? What crime has he committed?" asked Pilate.

But they shouted all the louder, "Crucify him!"

Acts 2:23: This man was handed over to you by God's deliberate plan and foreknowledge; and you, with the help of wicked men, put him to death by nailing him to the cross.

PONTIUS PILATE

When Pilate saw that he was getting nowhere, but that instead an uproar was starting, he took water and washed his hands in front of the crowd. "I am innocent of this man's blood," he said. "It is your responsibility!"

HUMANKIND

1 Peter 2:24: He himself bore our sins in his body on the tree, that we might die to sin and live to righteousness.

Isaiah 53:5: But he was pierced for our transgressions; he was crushed for our iniquities; upon him was the chastisement that brought us peace, and with his wounds we are healed.

GOD

2 Corinthians 5:21: God made him who had no sin to be sin for us, so that in him we might become the righteousness of God.

92. WAS THE LORD'S SUPPER A PASSOVER MEAL?

There is some question about whether the Lord's Supper was a Passover meal or a regular meal. The reason for the confusion is that Matthew, Mark, Luke, and John indicate that Jesus ate the meal the night before and was crucified on Preparation Day, which was also the day on which the Passover lamb was slain and eaten (Matthew 26:17–29; Matthew 27:62).

Both Mark and Luke clearly state that they were eating the Passover meal (Mark 14:12; Luke 22:7-8). However, John 18:28 indicates that the Jewish leaders hadn't yet eaten the Passover; in that case, how could Jesus have eaten it the night before? Did Jesus eat the Passover meal on the wrong day, or was it not a Passover meal?

The regulations for the Passover are set out in Exodus 12:1-30. The Passover lamb was to be slaughtered and eaten on the 14th day of the month, at twilight. And this does seem to be what takes place in the Gospels. If it wasn't for John's statement that the Jewish leaders wanted to be able to eat the Passover, it would be clear that on the first day of the Festival of Unleavened Bread, Jesus and his disciples ate the Passover meal, according to the scriptures.

So what do we do with John's statement? One explanation is that the Passover was the beginning of a seven-day Festival of Unleavened Bread, which was also sometimes called the Passover (Luke 2:41; Luke 22:1, 7; Acts 12:3–4). So the Jewish leaders had probably already eaten the Passover meal, just as Jesus and the disciples had. However, seven days remained of the Festival on which they would eat the prescribed unleavened bread along with other food. They would hold a sacred assembly and do no regular work, and they would offer a special burnt offering to the Lord (Leviticus 23:5-8; Numbers 28:16-25). It was for the festival activities that the Jewish leaders didn't want to be defiled (oh, the irony).

Therefore, John is actually in perfect harmony with Matthew, Mark, Luke, and John. All four identify the day Jesus died as the Day of Preparation, though John adds that it was the Day of Preparation of the Passover week (Much like we would say Easter

Sunday to identify the Sunday on which we celebrate that holiday.)

So there is actually no discrepancy at all. Jesus, his disciples, and all the other Jews ate the Passover meal on the first day of unleavened bread, which is the official day of Passover observance. The next day began the Festival of Unleavened Bread, and it was on this day that Jesus was crucified. This day, being the day before the Sabbath, is also known as Preparation Day (or Day of Preparation) because it was when the Jews made preparations to observe the Sabbath.

93. HOW LONG WAS JESUS ON THE CROSS?

Jesus was on the cross for six hours: from about 9am to 3pm.

First, it is important to note that there were two ways of telling time during this period. The Jews divided time into 12 hours, from sunrise to sunset. And starting from around 6am, they counted the first hour, second hour, third hour, etc. On the other hand, the Romans began keeping time starting at midnight, as Americans do now.

Here's a timeline beginning with Jesus' arrest in the Garden of Gethsemane:

1. Jesus is betrayed and arrested – **9pm to Midnight.**
2. Jesus appears before the high priest for his Jewish "trial" and Peter denies Jesus – **Midnight to 5am.**
3. The Sanhedrin declares Jesus guilty – **About 6am – daybreak.**
4. Jesus appears for his "trials" before Pilate and Herod, is beaten and mocked, and condemned to death – **6am to 8am.**
5. Jesus carries his cross to Golgotha with assistance from Simon of Cyrene – **Around 8am.**
6. Jesus is crucified along with two criminals – **9am (In some translations, Mark calls this the third hour – Mark 15:25).**
7. Darkness covers the land – **Noon to 3pm (the sixth to the ninth hour according to Mark 15 33).**
8. Jesus cries out and dies on the cross – **3pm (Mark 15:34-37).**

So we know how long Jesus was on the cross primarily because of Mark's account.

94. DID JESUS GO TO HELL BETWEEN HIS DEATH AND RESURRECTION?

No, Jesus never went to hell. When he died, he went to Hades or Sheol, which is a different place, according to Ephesians 4:8–10 and 1 Peter 3:18–20. He went there and took the believers with Him to heaven (Ephesians 4:8–10). Some of the confusion has arisen from such passages as Psalm 16:10–11, as translated in the King James Version:

> "For thou wilt not leave my soul in hell; neither wilt thou suffer thine Holy One to see corruption. . . . Thou wilt show me the path of life."

However, hell isn't a correct translation in this verse. A correct reading would be "the grave" or "Sheol." So the scripture is saying God wouldn't leave him in the grave.

95. AT JESUS' DEATH, WHAT WAS THE SIGNIFICANCE OF THE VEIL OF THE TEMPLE BEING TORN IN HALF?

The veil was a curtain in the temple that separated the holy place from the most holy place, where the Ark of the Covenant was kept. The only person who could enter the most holy place was the High Priest, and he could only enter once a year on the Day of Atonement, to atone for the sins of the people (Exod. 26:31–33; Lev. 16:12–15).

So the tearing of the veil at Jesus' death was pretty significant. It indicated that there was no longer a need for a High Priest to atone for sins on our behalf; Jesus' death accomplishes that once and for all. He is our High Priest! We no longer need a human mediator between ourselves and God.

96. HOW LONG WAS JESUS IN THE TOMB?

People have argued for years that Jesus wasn't really in the tomb "three days and three nights." However, this phrase was a popular way of speaking back then and wasn't necessarily meant to be taken literally.

Jesus was in the tomb for parts of three days: (1) Friday evening, (2) all day Saturday, and (3) part of the wee hours of Sunday morning.

Jews counted part of a day as one day, much as we do now. Suppose you go out of town sometime on Friday and come back Sunday evening. You are likely to say you had a three-day vacation. You don't say, "Now that's not technically three days. Let me get this right down to the minute so I can accurately tell people how long I was gone."

You naturally count each day as a full day in normal discussions, even if it wasn't the whole day. They did the same back in Jewish times. Again, Christians must stop making a big deal out of insignificant matters. The important thing is that Jesus died, and that he was buried, and that he was raised again on the third day. That's the central teaching of the Gospel.

97. WHO WERE THE WOMEN AT JESUS' CROSS/TOMB?

Mary, Jesus' mother, was at the cross. She wasn't in the company of the other women but was standing near the cross with the Apostle John (John 19:25-26). Since we don't hear about her again until the book of Acts, she likely went home with John after the crucifixion, as Jesus instructed, and did not go with the women to the tomb.

Mary Magdalene, **Mary the wife of Clopas**, and **Salome** watched the crucifixion some distance away from the cross (Matthew 27:55-56, Mark 15:40-41, Luke 23:48-49, John 25b).

These same women are listed as going to the tomb, with the addition of **Joanna** (Matthew 28:1-8, Mark 16:1-8, Luke 24:1-8, Luke 24:10, John 20:1). Joanna was likely at the crucifixion site, though she isn't named.

In addition, there were other unnamed women in the group.

98. HOW MANY ANGELS WERE AT JESUS' TOMB?

There were two angels at Jesus' tomb (Luke 24:1-8), but it seems that only one of them spoke, which is probably why Matthew (28:1-6) and Mark (16:1-7 only mention one angel. Listen, this is not a contradiction. It would only be a contradiction to say there was "only" one angel. But mentioning one without mentioning the other isn't a contradiction.

Matthew and Mark simply don't include all the information they could. But none of the Gospel writers include all the information for any given event. That's why it's helpful to have four Gospel witnesses regarding the events that took place. We learn more than if we relied only on one Gospel. Independent witnesses are always better than witnesses who say the same thing word for word.

99. IN WHAT ORDER DID JESUS APPEAR TO HIS FOLLOWERS AFTER HIS RESURRECTION?

After his resurrection, Jesus appeared to his followers in this order:

1. Mary Magdalene and the other women
2. Peter
3. Two of Jesus' followers on the road to Emmaus
4. 10 of the apostles in the locked room (Thomas was missing)
5. All 11 apostles (Remember Judas had committed suicide)
6. 7 of the apostles on the Sea of Galilee

7. More than 500 of his followers

100. WHY DIDN'T PEOPLE RECOGNIZE JESUS AFTER HE WAS RESURRECTED?

On numerous occasions after Jesus was resurrected, those closest to him didn't recognize him. The scriptures don't provide an explanation for this, but it's quite intriguing. Here are the instances where Jesus wasn't recognized:

A. Mary Magdalene when she encountered Jesus at the tomb (John 20:14-16)

B. The two disciples on the road to Emmaus (Luke 24:13-32)

C. The 12 disciples in the locked room. They didn't necessarily fail to recognize him; however, they thought he was a ghost (Luke 24:36-43)

D. Seven of the disciples on the Sea of Galilee (John 21:1-14)

The only logical conclusion is that Jesus' resurrected body had somehow changed significantly. And this actually agrees with the later teachings of the Bible.

For example, Paul goes into great detail to teach that when we are resurrected, we will be changed.

> But someone will ask, "How are the dead raised? With what kind of body will they come?" How foolish! What you sow does not come to life unless it dies. When you sow, you do not plant the body that will be, but just a seed, perhaps of wheat or of something else. But God gives it a body as he has determined, and to each kind of seed he gives its own body. Not all flesh is the same: People have one kind of flesh, animals have another, birds another and fish another. There are also heavenly bodies and there are earthly bodies; but the splendor of the heavenly bodies is one kind, and the splendor of the earthly bodies is another. The sun has one kind of splendor, the moon another and the stars another; and star differs from star in splendor.
>
> So will it be with the resurrection of the dead. The body that is sown is

perishable, it is raised imperishable; it is sown in dishonor, it is raised in glory; it is sown in weakness, it is raised in power; it is sown a natural body, it is raised a spiritual body. (1 Corinthians 15:35-44)

So when our perishable bodies are raised imperishable, our physical appearance will likely change. Thus, it seems that whatever happened to Jesus' body after his resurrection provides a glimpse of what will happen to our glorified bodies.

CONCLUSION

Jesus Christ is the most important person in the Bible, indeed, in the history of the world. Therefore, what we believe about him matters. And what we believe about him starts with what we know and understand about him.

I hope the answers in this book have cleared up any confusion surrounding the life of Jesus. I hope that you have had a new encounter with the King of kings and the Lord of Lords.

While none of us lived during biblical times, most of the information we seek is found right in the pages of the Bible, which is why this book is so scripture heavy.

If you have any questions this book didn't answer, please send them to the following email address:

jesusfaq@route66ministries.com

MORE BOOKS FROM C. AUSTIN TUCKER

If you enjoyed this book, you might also be interested in the below series.

Visit **amazon.com/author/caustintucker** for other books and for purchasing options.

ABOUT THE WORD TRUTH LIFE BIBLE

The Chronological Word Truth Life Bible is published by Route 66 Ministries, which is so named in reference to the 66 books of the Bible. The ministry is dedicated to encouraging people to encounter God through reading and understanding the Bible in chronological order.

Two scriptures in the Gospel of John inspired the "Word Truth Life" series title.

The Apostle John identifies Jesus as the **Word** (John 1:1, John 1:14), and Jesus identified himself as **the Way, the Truth, and the Life** (John 14:6). These adjectives not only apply to Jesus himself but to the book that illuminates him, the Bible.

The Word Truth Life Bible (WTLB) was born of the desire to provide a Bible version that's easier to read and understand than traditional Bibles. Many Christians know the familiar stories, but for many reasons they don't read the entire Bible to learn how everything fits together. Some of the most common reasons for this are:

> The Bible is big.
> The Bible is confusing.
> The Bible is boring.

The WTLB solves these issues. Although there will be many differences in comparison with traditional Bibles, Route 66 Ministries is committed not only to acknowledging the full and complete authority of Scripture but also remaining true to its entire message.

Therefore, despite its different packaging, unique formatting, and shorter length, none of the Bible's content is missing. This has been the main concern in undertaking such a project.

ABOUT C. AUSTIN TUCKER

C. Austin Tucker is a writer, editor, and teacher with a passion for God and his Word. She has been a Bible teacher for more than 20 years and is the founder of Route 66 Ministries, which is dedicated to helping people read and understand the Bible chronologically. She holds a Master's Degree in Biblical Studies and plans to pursue a doctorate. When not writing, she's most likely indulging in old-school music and sitcoms or watching superhero and time travel movies.

Connect with her at CAustinTucker@Route66Ministries.com or **Facebook.com/Route66Ministries**

www.ingramcontent.com/pod-product-compliance
Lightning Source LLC
Chambersburg PA
CBHW060323050426
42449CB00011B/2617